Prison City Kiddie

Ken Colbo

Dedications

To Father Jack Murray, for his inspiration, guidance, and friendship.

About the Author

Ken lives in Lolo, Montana, and is a lifelong Montanan. He loves to mountain bike, cross-country ski, golf, hike into mountain lakes, and play losing chess with his friends. He's now retired after two careers in education and financial planning. He graduated from Montana State University with a BA and an MA.

Table of Contents

PROLOGUE

Over the years, many of my friends have often said that I should write a book. Why, I ask them? Because a lot of weird stuff has happened to you, is the most common response. The second most common was, because you are a goofball! I'm not quite sure what a goofball is, but now I think I must be one. A lot of stuff that could be in the prologue is in the Introduction, so that's it!

INTRODUCTION
"Prison City Kiddie"

Just who is the Prison City Kiddie? It's me – Kenneth Gordon Colbo, Jr. By the way, no one ever called me Junior and for that I've been eternally grateful. I have been called a lot of other things and a lot of those weren't very flattering.

On March 21, 1942, at 3:00 A.M., I popped out into the world, a whopping six pounds and two ounces. My first days were spent in a tiny hospital in Deer Lodge, Montana. In the future, I would be readmitted into this little two-story building to have my tonsils removed, which wasn't bad as I got to suck on a bunch of popsicles. My next stay was to get rid of pneumonia, again not a big deal. It just seemed like a bad cold. Next, I went there for my first hernia operation. It was horrible! I threw up for three days, thanks to ether. I was let go after two weeks, hoping my little nut would stay where it was supposed to be, you know, in the sac. Worse yet, the operation didn't work, and I had to go to St. Pat's Hospital in Missoula twice to get my wandering testicle to stay in its intended place – more about testicles later.

Deer Lodge's real claim to fame is that Montana's territorial prison was located on the west end of its main street. The Prison was a haunting sight with twenty-foot-high walls that were fourteen feet thick, made out of large rocks and cement. A tough-as-nails warden, whose last name was Conley, made the prisoners build the prison – talk about saving the taxpayers money! When anyone found out that I was from Deer Lodge, they would frequently ask me if I was afraid to live only blocks away from the prison. My response was: "Do you really think if a prisoner could get over the twenty-foot walls that he would just hang out in Deer Lodge?" Most of the time, they would go to Butte, the closest "bigger" town, get drunk, write some bad checks, and eventually return to their home away from home – Montana State Prison.

Deer Lodge sits at the base of Mount Powell, a beautiful ten-thousand-foot mountain located in the Deer Lodge National Forest. The wide valley below Mount Powell is home to several cattle ranches, potato farms, and quite a few wheat farms. About five thousand people lived in Deer Lodge at the time, not counting the two thousand convicts.

What made Deer Lodge tick? For starters, the Milwaukee Railroad out of Chicago had a large shop on the west side of town that employed about four hundred railroaders. Their job was to repair broken train parts and engines. One of the perks of working at the shops was the opportunity to bring home wrenches, shovels, hammers, ball bearings and a lot of other useful stuff. Not all the railroaders participated in these endeavors, but a lot of them did. Potlicker Brown and Dead Eye Newbauer worked at the shops – more about these characters later.

One hundred men worked in the phosphate mines that were located near Garrison and Avon. Garrison was about ten miles from Deer Lodge and Avon was about twenty miles away. Phosphate sounds like it might be a soft rock, but it's not! It's hard as hell! I worked at the Luke for a few months. We worked about two thousand feet below ground level. A lot of miners had really short life spans, as many of them died from black lung disease. Later, I'll tell you what it's like to go underground.

Somewhere around one hundred Deer Lodgers commuted to Butte and Anaconda to work in the copper mines in Butte and the refinery in Anaconda. Butte citizens call their town "Butte America." They also call it the "holy" city because of the humongous holes the mines created by doing open pit mining. The biggest hole is the Berkeley Pit, which is one mile long by one half mile wide and around 1780 feet deep. Now, that's a real hole!

Butte people have their own unique language called "Buchian." They always greet you by saying: "How's she going?" never "How's it going?" In my opinion, they are the best people on earth. They are survivors in the best sense of the word.

Anaconda is famous for having the tallest surviving masonry structure in the world. Its refinery smokestack is 555 feet tall. The junk spewing out of the stack killed off most of the trees and vegetation for miles around Anaconda. The refinery closed down decades ago, and finally, the trees and vegetation are coming back after millions and millions of dollars have been spent to try to fix the harm done to the environment because of the mines and the refinery. For decades, the Clark Fork River, flowing through Deer Lodge, was colored orange and brown. Orange because of the arsenic and brown because of the open sewage being piped into it by the farmers and ranchers whose land was next to the river. No one with any sense would step into this river, let alone eat a fish that swam in it.

Finally, because of the many forests near Deer Lodge, a lot of loggers found homes in the prison city. The loggers were a bunch of tough hombres. The consensus was that Snore Newbauer was the meanest logger and Tom "the Russian" was the worst dude of all the miners. We all thought that if they ever fought one another, it would be a sight to behold.

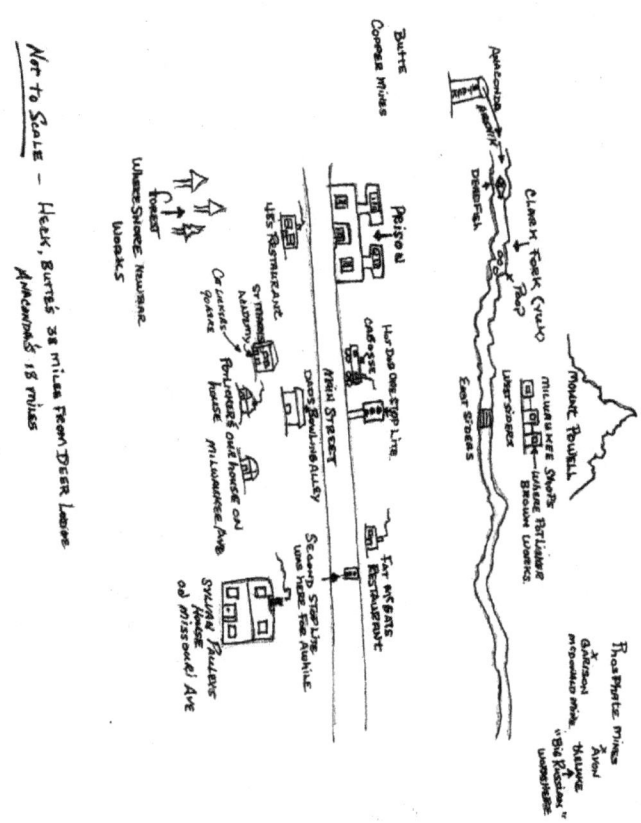

I thought it would be a good idea to draw a map of Deer Lodge to show you where things were and also to make it more than obvious that I'm not an artist.

CHAPTER 1

Life On a Turkey, Chicken, Rabbit, Potato & Two Cow Farm

I could easily write an entire book about my father, who was quite amazing. Dad was raised on a little homestead outside of Baker, Montana. Baker is located in eastern Montana and is almost in North Dakota. Around Baker is a whole lot of dust, sagebrush, snakes and gopher holes. At best, it is a barren, harsh land.

Dad's father was a tough, stubborn German whose idea of work was to work until you were totally exhausted. So, you worked from sunup to sundown, seven days a week. He was about six feet tall and had a presence about him that no one wanted to challenge. Because of his common sense and honesty, he was elected to the State Senate. My dad worshipped his father. Dad was thirteen when his dad died at the age of 43 from a tick bite.

Dad hardly knew his mother. She died from the flu when he was six. As if that wasn't bad enough, his sister died at an early age by falling into a stream and drowning. When Dad started high school, he was the smallest boy, by far, in his class. He wasn't quite five feet tall. His stepmother made him stay home to do chores on the farm, at least as much as she could get away with. He got by because he was pretty darn smart. He just didn't grow very much and was only five feet two inches tall when he graduated from high school.

Dad's dream growing up was to stay on the farm and work on it for the rest of his life. Sadly, when he turned eighteen, his evil stepmother (literally) disinherited him and told him he had to leave the farm. He only had eight dollars to his name, the clothes on his back, and a cardboard suitcase with an advertisement for a grocery store plastered on the inside of the top lid. It would be the only suitcase my father ever owned.

My father and three of his friends, who were barely surviving, joined in his exodus out of Baker. He told me that they had twenty-eight dollars amongst them. The one thing they knew was that they were going to head West. They had no clue where they were going to stop. "West" promised to have forests, rivers and grassy meadows. Anything had to be better than where they were leaving.

Traveling with Dad was Swede Perriman and the two Robbins brothers. An old Model T Ford was their means of transportation. All of them were confident they could find some kind of work because they all were really "Jack of All Trades" types. They all could run any kind of farm machinery, ride horses, milk cows, and fix just about anything with some wire and a pair of pliers.

They continued driving West in the old Model T Ford until they saw the Pauley Ranch located in the valley below Mount Powell. The ranch was started by a remarkable sheepherder – Silvan Pauley. He saved every nickel he made and started buying land and cattle when he could. At its zenith, the ranch was the second largest in the continental United States. Only the King Ranch in Texas was larger. A beautiful stream named Rock Creek ran through the 130,000-acre ranch.

Dad worked on the ranch for about a year and then moved into Deer Lodge to work as a butcher at the territorial prison. Swede joined Dad in going to Deer Lodge, becoming a carpenter, and eventually owning a small farm just outside the city limits of Deer Lodge. The Robbins brothers stayed on the ranch the rest of their lives. The ranch owners made them foremen and gave them each five acres of land and a house to live in. Howard Robbins died at Age 84 and his brother Newt lived to Age 96.

Pop always wanted to be a farmer, so he saved enough money to put a down payment on a ten-acre farm just two miles east of Deer Lodge. My first memories were being on the farm as a three-year-old. Thanks for hanging in there – the interesting, fun stuff is coming up.

My Mom was born on a small ranch about ten miles from Helena, the capitol of Montana. Her father was a double-tough French-Canadian cowboy, gambler, politician, bare-knuckled fighter, who deserves a full chapter in this book. Our family always believed that there might have been some teepee creeping going on because Mom's mother sat on the floor and smoked a pipe. Mom's very dark brown eyes were a giveaway.

When Mom was eleven, good old gramps gave her his 45 pistol to shoot some gophers. Talk about overkill! She held it too close to her face, so when she fired, the recoil broke her nose and gave her two black eyes. Growing up, I discovered that Mom was the real athlete in the family. She would go with me to catch some fish, gun down some ducks, or shoot some gophers. You may have guessed by now; my family called an all-out war on these little rodents.

I spent many hours playing catch with my mom. She had a great arm. I avoided playing catch with my dad because he was lousy at throwing and was worse at catching a hardball. As my arm got stronger, and I pitched American Legion baseball, I was afraid I might hit him in the noggin and kill him.

This brings me to my first memories of living on a tiny farm with a very strict, stubborn German father and a really cool French Canadian, Scotch, Irish and Native American mother. Also, I had a brother thirteen months older than I was (Keith), who I followed around the farm. If he suddenly stopped, I would bump into him.

One of my first and favorite memories was getting a cap gun, which was given to me by my favorite Aunt Ellen when I was three or four. It was the real deal, a Roy Rogers six-shooter. The holster had some silver stars on it. I pretended to shoot and destroy every turkey on the farm.

We lived in a tiny white house with only three rooms in it. My brother and I shared a bedroom space that was not more than eight feet wide and ten feet long. Our little nest was separated from the rest of the house by a green blanket hung from the ceiling. Mom and Dad had their own bedroom. The rest of the house served as a kitchen and a tiny living room. When I was four years old, it seemed like it was plenty big enough.

Dad was raising about fifty turkeys on the farm. I hated those mean feathered monsters. When you're really little, and you have to navigate your way around them, and you were pretty sure they all wanted to peck you to death, you become a lifelong, full-fledged turkey hater. I was told that turkeys are so dumb that they would raise their beaks up to drink in a rainstorm and drown. I'm not sure that's true, but I always wanted it to be.

In the middle of summer, I followed my brother around as usual, when I somehow managed to climb up to look into a very slimy horse trough. I fell in. I started drinking way too much horse water. Lucky for me, my brother thought it was funny and started laughing his little butt off. His sense of humor saved my life. Don Hunt, my dad's hired hand, saw my brother looking into the trough and laughing, and ran over to see what was so funny. Don yanked me out and pushed on my chest until a little geyser of water spurted out of me. A few more seconds of consuming horse water and Kenneth Gordon Colbo Jr. would have been in the happy hunting grounds. I think that is heaven because I wasn't old enough to earn my way into keeping company with the devil.

Shortly after that episode, Keith and I decided it would be fun to chop up a wooden box. Our tools of destruction were my little hammer and his really sharp hoe. Taking turns hitting the box, one of us got out of turn, and my little "big brother" hit me on top of my head with the hoe. He hit me hard enough to slice through my little purple beanie with a yellow propeller on top of it and put a gash in my noggin. I covered my beanie with my hands so the blood wouldn't run down my face, then I ran into the house. When I got inside, I took my hands down and a bunch of blood ran down my face. Mom almost passed out. Dad asked what happened and when I told him, he dashed outside to spank my brother. I yelled that it wasn't his fault, but it really was … sort of. Mom bandaged me as best she could, and Dad took me into town to see the doctor. I think it took about forty stitches to close the wound.

I promised my folks that I would be more careful in the future. I decided it would be best if I stayed away from turkeys, horse troughs, and my brother, if he had any kind of sharp implement in his hands.

For about six weeks, I was good to go, and then I got the bright idea that it would be fun to climb to the top of a big old cottonwood tree. I think Darwin was probably right about humans being part monkey, because I had little trouble climbing to the top. All was swell, and then, for some unknown reason, I decided I could wrap my legs around a branch and hang upside down. Fortunately for me, this idea didn't enter my mind until I was only about eight feet off the ground. I soon found out that humans aren't possums when my legs gave out and I crashed into the ground head-first. This was the first of many concussions that I would experience in my lifetime. In those days, if you had a concussion, they locked you in a dark room for three or four days. So, I had a pretty good idea of what convicts went through when they were put into the hole (solitary confinement) for their misdeeds.

Convicts were only fed bread and water; at least, I was fed soup and water and a few cookies. I added trees to the list of things I should avoid in the future.

CHAPTER 2

Sisters of Charity "Sometimes"

Because of turkey pecking, swimming in horse troughs, being beaned in my beanie, and cottonwood crashing, I don't remember any more of my fifth year on this planet. Try as he might, Dad just couldn't make ends meet on the farm, so we moved into town. When I was six, we lived in a two-story grey house on Second Street. The bottom floor was a little grocery store and we lived on the upper floor for about six months. I was in candy bar heaven. I was no doubt partially responsible for us having to move to another house in about six months. We would move two more times in the next two years before landing at 930 Milwaukee Avenue, where my folks would live the rest of their lives. In Deer Lodge, if you had a little money, you lived on Milwaukee Avenue, and if you were loaded, you lived on Missouri Avenue. Silvan Pauley lived on Missouri Avenue.

Our grocery store house was only four blocks below St. Mary's Academy, run by the Sisters of Charity. Mom, being Catholic, enrolled me into the first grade at the Academy. It sounds like an absolutely adorable place to begin my education. I would soon learn the nuns were sometimes less than charitable and, in fact, some were mean as hell.

I remember my first day of school like it was yesterday. I wore a brand-new snazzy pair of tan corduroy pants and an orange shirt. I thought I looked pretty darn good! My first-grade teacher was a rather nice-looking, slightly overweight nun, named Sister Zeta. The thing I'll always remember were her fingernails. They were really long and very sharp! I'm left-handed, so it was natural for me to use my left hand to print and to write. Sister Zeta was bound and determined that I would use my right hand when writing. The second time she caught me using my left hand, she grabbed me by my neck just under my chin and pinched me really hard. She broke the skin on my neck, and I started to bleed onto my shirt. When I arrived home after school, I didn't want to get into trouble, so I fibbed to my mom and said that I got into a fight with one of the Burdick brothers and he cut my neck a little bit. Mom seemed to buy my story. About three days later, Sister Zeta caught me writing left-handed and pinched my neck again. It was bleeding, darn it. I dreaded going home – I just knew I was going to get spanked for causing trouble at school. Mom looked at me and said: "What happened to your neck, and this time you had better tell me the truth." So, I hold her what happened. I was amazed to see how fast my mom ran by me to get out the back door and into her car. She sped out of our driveway, throwing gravel all over the place. My part Native American mother was on the warpath. I don't know what Mom said to Sister Zeta, but from that day forward, I could write left-handed. In fact, Sister Zeta never even looked at me for the rest of the school year.

The public-school kids called us Catholics, cat-lickers. We countered by calling them pup-lickers. About ninety of us cat-lickers attended St. Mary's Academy. Thirty of the ninety were orphans. I'm not sure if the orphans licked cats or not. The principal of the school was Sister Bernard. She made Bronco Nagurski look like a midget. Bronco played fullback for the Chicago Bears and worse a size 21 ring. You could put a silver dollar through it. Now, that is a big finger! That's how big I thought Sister Bernard was. She ran the Academy with an iron fist.

We didn't have a lot of playground equipment, so we entertained ourselves during recess by playing games like "touched you last." It was really bad if you got touched last before recess ended and you had to get back to class. "Smear the Queer" was also fun. You threw rubber balls at one another. If you couldn't catch the ball, you were out of the game. Nicer, more sophisticated people called it "Dodgeball."

We did have some monkey bars that became my favorite recess entertainment. Below is a drawing that shows what monkey bars look like for those of you who don't know.

After falling out of a tree onto my noggin, I wasn't about to let go of the bars. We would start at each end of the bars and proceed to the center, going from one bar to another until we could get close enough to wrap our legs around our opponent. Then, you tugged as hard as you could until one of you hit the ground. I was monkey bar champion in my class for four consecutive years. If Sister Bernard could climb the monkey bar steps, she would have pulled the whole contraption down.

Most of the time, we just chased one another around and threw things at each other. In the six grade, Tony Burdick, my best friend and a real screwball, and I became aware that girls would leave their bathroom door open a little bit, so we had a line of sight into it. Tony and I decided it would be a good idea to bring binoculars to school to get a better view. Apparently, Sister Bernard was watching us watching them. She ran toward us looking like a runaway locomotive. She hauled us up to her office. She hit me with a large book in the back of my head. I was knocked off my feet. Tony got the same treatment, but managed to stay on his feet. Next comes the best part – she proceeded to go into great detail about how we were going to be severely burned on a daily basis in the fires of hell. We tried to tell her that we really didn't see anything bad, but she didn't seem to care. Finally, she marched us across the street to see the Parish Priest, Father Moran. I would spend a lot of time going to confession.

The next part of the book comes with a warning. It is not for someone with a weak stomach. Consider yourself warned!

There was an orphan girl in the sixth grade whose name was Ann. Ann looked like a combination of Ichabod Crane and Abe Lincoln. Actually, she didn't look that good, and to my credit, I always tried to be nice to her. Now to the bad part: Ann almost every day would pick her long nose and eat her boogers. I warned you! Tony and I would make small bets who could watch the longest without looking away. Happily, I always lost. You're no doubt going to recover from reading this as you didn't witness this spectacle first-hand.

During my time at the academy, I met Jack Murray, who was five years older than I was. Jack taught me how to be an altar boy. He went on to become a priest. I don't have the words to tell you how much I admire Father Jack. He taught me a lot more about how to block and tackle in football than any of my coaches. I started hiking into mountain lakes with Jack when I was about 11 years old. During my lifetime, I have hiked with Jack to more than a hundred mountain lakes. He possesses enormous stamina and can hike incredible distances. Several years ago, he hiked the Camino de Santiago three times. He treated the thousand miles like it was a walk in the park.

Father Jack took the Vow of Poverty seriously. By far, his favorite place to shop was thrift stores. Any time we went hiking, he would always ask me how much I paid for my hiking gear. He would proudly state that his gear cost about 95% less than what I had paid for my stuff.

Jack loved to hike into mountain lakes in Glacier Park. Glacier Park is notorious for having a large population of grizzly bears. I wondered why Jack never encountered a grizzly in his hundreds of miles of hiking into the park. While hiking into a mountain lake in the Deer Lodge National Forest, I found out the hard way. We were just above a lake when we saw some fresh bear tracks. It was raining that day, so the tracks were easy to see. Without any warning, good old Jack let out the most blood-curdling scream I have ever heard. I would have rather wrestled that bear than listen to that scream again. It's a wonder that all of the bears in Glacier didn't run out of the park and go north into Canada. Father Jack is now 85 years old and he has pancreatic cancer. He is on his second round of chemo treatments. If anyone can survive cancer, it will be Father Jack Murray.

Many times, when I thought about doing something inappropriate, I asked myself if I would do that if Father Jack were here. The answer was always, 'No'.

Thanks to Father Jack, I was serving the Good Lord as an altar boy, because I always rang the little bell and genuflected at the correct time. Father Moran wanted me to serve mass a lot. So, I got to serve mass at a ton of weddings and funerals. I hate funerals to this day, having had to look into approximately one hundred open caskets containing a lot of old people who I knew in town. It gave me the heebie-jeebies to look at their cold, lifeless, wrinkled bodies, plastered with all kinds of powder and make-up so they didn't look so dead. They still looked real dead. Even worse, I hardly ever got any tips for serving mass at funerals.

Weddings were a different story. People getting married weren't dead yet, and even better, I got some big tips from the happy couples. We made little side-bets on how long we thought the marriages would last.

Around Thanksgiving time, all of us cat-lickers had to sell raffle tickets, with the winners getting some prizes. I won almost every year because I had an ace in the hole, so to speak. The ace was Potlicker Brown's wife, Mrs. Potlicker. Mrs. Potlicker weighed, just guessing, over four hundred pounds. The Potlickers lived in a log cabin just two blocks from our house. The log cabin was heated with a large wood stove that Mrs. P. was always sitting by, usually eating potato chips. I loved Mrs. Potlicker because she would buy ten dollars' worth of $.25 tickets. That number of tickets almost guaranteed me a win. I kept it a secret where my honey pot was.

In the fourth grade, I suddenly got the urge to play the piano. That looked like fun. Sister Josephine was my instructor. I must have been a hopeless case because she smacked me on my hands with a yard stick about every thirty seconds for messing up. I endured the so-called lessons for two weeks and only learned how to move my hands away from the piano really quickly. I did learn that I had no future as a musician. I also recall that I was part of a huge production that required dressing up as a monkey. I guess the play might have been about Darwin. I don't remember, but the costume seemed to fit my day-to-day behavior, especially my expertise on the monkey bars.

To be honest, not all of the nuns were mean. I actually received a good education at St. Mary's Academy. My second-grade teacher was an avid baseball fan. She had us keep a scrapbook about a major league baseball team. I picked the Boston Red Sox and have been a fan of the Sox ever since. She was way cool and let us listen to the World Series on the radio.

Also, Sister Bernard wasn't nearly as large as I made her out to be. When you're little, everything seems bigger to you. I don't want to eliminate any chance of going to Heaven. Hey, I believe in miracles.

Every now and then, the pup-lickers' basketball coach would invite us little cat-lickers to come over and play basketball. We could beat them, much to their dismay. Three of us lickers of cats were asked to join them, the public school's junior high basketball team. Not quite five feet tall, I was an imposing figure. Also, I was sort of on the chubby side. I had a running hook shot that seldom went in, but when it did, it was a sight to behold.

The one game I will always remember was against Anaconda's Junior High. Watching them warm up, I noticed that I had a really tall, sort of fat kid to guard. He was about five feet eight and weighed well over two hundred pounds. I told my buddies that I couldn't wait to guard him. I was going to steal the ball from him – no sweat! The first time this heavy-set kid came up the floor toward me, I was licking my chops just knowing that I would take the ball away from him. I was ready to make my move when he dribbled the ball behind his back and headed toward the basket, leaving me with my mouth open in amazement. Not only that, but he swished a twenty-foot jump shot. As near as I can remember, Chubby Kid scored about fifty points and Anaconda beat us like a drum. He was only a seventh grader.

Every year, that chubby boy grew two or three inches taller and stayed the same weight, until he graduated from high school at 6'7" and about 240 pounds. His name was Wayne Estes. He went on the play for Utah State, was an All-American, and was considered to be the best college basketball player in America. On February 8, 1965, after his last college game, in which Wayne scored 48 points, he and some of his friends stopped at the scene of a car accident near campus. While crossing the street, Wayne brushed against a powerline and was electrocuted. His six-foot friend walked underneath the power line with no problem.

While playing little league and Babe Ruth baseball, when pitching against Anaconda, I threw a lot of curveballs to Wayne. He no doubt hit many of them really hard. Oftentimes, his father and my father would umpire our games. They became good friends. Damn, I wished he had never stopped to help on that fatal night. To this day, I think of him and say a prayer for him.

That's about it for my grade school days, other than drinking a tiny bit of whiskey with my buddy Tony at St. Mary's Academy's graduation picnic. We poured it into Kool-Aid cups. It struck me that people who liked drinking whiskey must also like drinking kerosene. Tony and I almost always got caught messing up, but on this fine day we flew under the radar. I proudly graduated with a minute amount of honor and was sure that if I was doing anything in the future that was fun, it was probably a sin.

CHAPTER 3

"Sex Education Learned While Setting Pins in a Bowling Alley"

After Dad sold the neighborhood grocery store, he came up with another idea of how to strike it rich. He found out that there were a bunch of abandoned railroad cars sitting out in a field just collecting dust. Don't ask me how he did it, but he managed to haul one over Westside Bridge and onto Main Street. He found a great spot across the street from the post office.

There was enough room in the railroad car for a counter, eight stools, and three narrow tables. At the far end of the railroad car was a small stove and a cupboard filled with dishes and eating utensils. Dad sold hot dogs for 25¢ and hamburgers for 50¢. A glass of root beer was 20¢. It seemed like he was doing a lot of business because every night, he brought home a canvas bag filled with coins, some as large as a dollar.

A lot of times, I would walk from home down to the caboose to help clean up a little, run some errands, and hope I would be rewarded with a hot dog and some root beer. A hamburger was a little too much to hope for.

While running the caboose hot dog stand, Pop found out that there was a bowling alley in Anaconda that would give away, for free, their worn-out bowling lanes if someone would just come and haul them away. Across the street from the hot dog caboose was a long narrow brick building that dad measured to make sure he could fit in four lanes. I'll never know how he thought about a bowling alley, for, as far as I knew, he didn't know how to bowl. Why would he haul four worn out lanes to Deer Lodge? My Dad was pretty darn smart and very, very practical. He turned the lanes upside down because the bottoms were as good as new. I would never have thought of that, and neither did the former owner.

In the front part of the building, Dad put in a soda fountain that became a small restaurant. In her tiny kitchen at home, Mom baked about ten pies and six cakes a day for sale at the fountain. Most were pre-sold. Mom was a heck of a cook. No wonder I was called pie face.

The fountain was a popular hang-out for high school kids. Dad would not let anyone swear in his establishment. If he heard anyone cursing, out they went. Everyone was afraid to mess with my father, so guess what? A lot of times, they took it out on me. Many a time, the cursers would wait for me to walk around the building to go in the back door to set pins. Sometimes, I would walk two or three extra blocks to avoid them. Sometimes, when they caught me, they would hold me down and thump my chest. On one side of the building, there were steps that led to a basement. At the top of the steps, there was a railing to keep people from falling into the basement. To me, it seemed like a thirty-foot drop. I dreaded getting caught on that side of the building. The big tough high school snots would hang me upside down by my ankles and tell me they were going to let go of me, so I could land on my head at the landing. I warned them that I wouldn't stay little forever and that I would get even with them. And I did! It suddenly stopped happening. I knew Dad found out about it.

Dear old Dad told me what a tough little bugger I was, and had me start setting pins when I was all of nine years old. I would manage to pick up one pin at a time and had barely enough strength to pull down the rack holding the ten pins. Bowling pins in those days weighed about four pounds. I finally stopped setting pins when I was a sophomore in high school because we got automatic pinsetters. I could pick up five pins at a time by then. One of the happiest days of my life was when I found out we were getting automatic pinsetters that would be installed in Dad's new eight-lane bowling alley. Even better, it didn't have a fountain or restaurant in it.

Sometimes, I had to lift forty-pound boxes of pins above my head to place them on a shelf for storage. I'm pretty darn sure that's why I had to have my first hernia operation when I was twelve.

My first hernia operation was done in Deer Lodge. My testicle stayed put for about six months and then went back up into my stomach again. If you have never had a testicle go up into your stomach, for those of you who haven't, I can assure you it hurts like hell. The next two Christmases, I was sent to St. Patrick Hospital in Missoula to do two more hernia operations. Dad didn't want me missing school because of a little testicular problem. I offered the pain up to the good Lord so a lot of my sins could be forgiven. I actually thought I had some credit up there. After the three surgeries, my left nut looked like someone took it out and played pool with it. I was sure I would never produce any children, but surprise, surprise, I have three daughters!

Next, to the sex education part of life in a bowling alley. O boy, O boy! One of Dad's pinsetters was a twenty-something old man whose first name was Bart. Because he passed an incredible amount of gas, naturally, I called him Bart the Fart. Not to his face, of course. Bart was about six feet tall and weighed well over two hundred pounds.

Bart felt compelled to pass on to me his vast knowledge in the sex education field. In between farts, he told me the first thing I had to know about females was, pointing to his nut-sack, that there are three things down there for your little wiener and if your little wiener gets in the wrong area, you will never be able to pee again. I sure wanted to keep on peeing, so I simply had to figure out the right thing down there. For a couple of years, I frequently wondered about what was down there. Bart made it sound awfully dangerous. I finally got up enough nerve to go to the library to find out what's what. After a great deal of searching, I found an anatomy book. Lo and behold, I discovered there were only a couple of things to worry about which greatly improved my odds of being able to continue peeing.

Actually, Bart gave me some good advice. He said: "A farting horse will never tire; a farting man is the man to hire." Being the expert farter that Bart was, I believed him, and I was sure Bart would never be out of a job. As I got older, I was around many other pinsetters who could offer me some sex education advice, but none of them could hold a candle to Bart!

I loved to set pins for Dead Eye Newbauer. He wasn't called Dead Eye because he was a good shot. He was about 6'4" and weighed a solid 260 pounds – he was a massive dude. Dead Eye liked to get lit up at the Corner Bar and then bowl a few lines. His idea of bowling was to see how hard he could throw the ball, hoping he could shatter a few pins. He couldn't care less about his score. Why in the world did I like to set pins for him? He would leave me a dollar for two hours of setting pins, and at Christmas, he would leave five dollars which seemed like a fortune.

When I set pins in the springtime, I would leave the back door open to get some fresh air because just about all of the bowlers smoked. The bowling alley only had one fan that blew all of the smoke toward us. During leagues, it was so smokey that we couldn't tell who threw the ball. The back door was about three feet off the ground. I had to crawl up to get onto the bench to set pins. The lane that Dead Eye chose to bowl was located directly in front of the open back door. I knew if the head pin was still standing and there were pins left standing behind it, that pins could fly up and hit me in the legs. Not wanting to get hit, I would pull my legs up just before the pins were about to fly.

Dead Eye wound up and fired the sixteen-pound ball that looked like a black missile heading toward my little body. Ka pow! Pins went flying. My legs shot into the air. A pin flew into the edge of the bench

I was sitting on and ricocheted into my face, knocking me ass over tea kettle out the back door and into a mud puddle in the road behind the bowling alley. My brother, who was setting pins next to me yelled at my dad, who was keeping score up front: "Gordy (my middle name) flew out the back door." Later, they told me dad ran down the lane, slid under the rack and jumped over the bench and landed by my soggy body in the mud puddle. He looked me over and asked if I was okay. I don't remember what I said, but I must have mumbled something that made him think I was okay because he stood me up. My face was starting to swell, and my nose was broken, teeth were knocked into the roof of my mouth and blood was coming out of my ears. Dad said, "looks like you're going to live; go up front to the fountain, get some aspirin, have a Coke." "I'll set pins for you for about twenty minutes, then come back here and finish setting pins for Dead Eye." I remember thinking how cool it was to have my father setting pins for me. Dad sure didn't want to raise a spoiled son. It took about thirty minutes to finish up setting pins for good old Dead Eye. My face and head really hurt. I walked over to the dentist's office first. Luckily, he was only two blocks away. Later, I found out that Dead Eye felt so bad that he almost killed me that he gave my dad a five-dollar bill to give to me.

I absolutely hated to go to the dentist. He had the worst breath in North America. I guess there was a guy in South America whose breath was so bad he could kill a medium size reptile by breathing on it. The rich people in Deer Lodge got to go to the other dentist, whom I was told had okay breath. After two hours and a lot of pain, the dentist, because I kept scooting down the dentist chair, peeled me off the floor and sent me on my merry way. Next, I headed over to the doctor's office, which was only three blocks away. Who says there aren't advantages of living in a small town? Doc Anderson checked me over and said I had a concussion and a broken nose, which he put an aluminum guard over and told me I was good to go. Head throbbing, I walked home knowing I had to be put in a dark bedroom for a few days. My mom had a completely different idea of how my noggin should have been cared for. Only thirteen more concussions to go.

Setting pins, I made a whopping 8¢ a line. So, for about two hours of ducking flying pins, lifting bowling balls that would mess up my own balls and inhaling second-hand smoke, I could earn about a dollar. After my first week of pin setting, Dad paid me. I was pretty good at math, so I checked the numbers and I saw that I was only paid 7¢ a line. I very, very carefully mentioned this to my dad. He told me that he took out a penny a line to send into Social Security. "What's that?" "It is for your retirement. The government requires me to pay into this program." I decided then and there that I didn't like the Government.

Over the years, I haven't changed that feeling very much. I just think, for 8¢, if a bowler bowled a 150 game, about average, I would have to pick up 585 lbs. of pins and approximately 288 lbs. of bowling balls. Somehow, that doesn't seem fair. However, after two years of setting pins, I got a raise of 2¢ a line. Now we were talking big money!

The happiest day of my young life was when, in my sophomore year in high school, Pop built a brand new eight-lane bowling alley that was going to have automatic pinsetters. No more setting pins until midnight. The only thing I missed was that while Dad was closing up, he would fix me a hamburger and sometimes, I could also have a chocolate sundae. And one more thing – if I was getting tired or I didn't like the bowlers, I would take his ball from alley one or two and send it back on alley three or four. I'm damn glad that not one of the bowlers I messed with told my dad about my indiscretions. Just one more thing to talk about in confession.

CHAPTER 4

Grandpa Coty

My grandpa Burt Coty was a real critter. He arrived in the Helena Valley from Montreal, Canada, sometime in the early nineteen hundreds. Helena is the capitol city of Montana. The Gold Rush was in full swing at the time. Helena's main street was named Last Chance Gulch. Grandpa was a raw-boned, wiry six-foot French Canadian. His eyes were dark brown, and it seemed like they could see right through you. His roman nose, square jaw and snow-white hair made him ruggedly handsome. He could have been a taller twin brother to Gus, the famous Texas Ranger played by Robert Duvall in the movie Lonesome Dove.

Grandpa couldn't say a word without using his hands to get his point across. I swear if you held his arms down, he wouldn't have been able to say a word. I never saw him without his flat wide-brimmed cowboy hat perched on his noggin and that included inside the house.

I always wondered if he wore it to bed. Anytime he saw a group of men, he always greeted them by saying, "Good morning, ladies."

He was a great storyteller, who told jokes (mostly off-color) to anyone who would listen. He seemed to get a big kick out of telling jokes to priests. Even on his deathbed, he managed to tell one to the priest who was giving him last rites.

One of his friends was the famous western artist, Charlie Russell, whom he met in one of the Last Chance Gulch's watering holes. I guess because of his ability to easily make friends, he was elected to be a County Commissioner. He was a lifelong Democrat and Grandma was a Republican. They cancelled out each other's votes for the seventy years they were married.

Grandpa started each day by drinking a water glass full of Seagram Seven whiskey with some sugar in it. He said it was mouthwash and if anyone was nearby, he would gargle it a bit before he put it down the hatch. Besides his love for booze, he liked to play poker. He somehow managed to save enough money to purchase a small ranch 20 miles west of Helena. It was a beautiful ranch with large meadows and a pretty stream running through it.

One night, good old Gramps went into Helena to play poker. He had no business being in a game of high stakes poker with players that had a ton more money than he had. He managed to lose thirteen thousand dollars that he didn't have to a very wealthy man who owned several bakeries in Montana. So, with his tail between his legs, he arrived home at three o'clock in the morning to face Grandma with the bad news. According to Grandma, he told her that he had some good news and some bad news. "Well, what's the bad news?" "We have to sell the ranch to pay off the bakery guy, because I lost thirteen thousand dollars to him." After almost passing out, she asked him what could possibly be the good news? Grandpa said: "We now get a chance to travel."

Grandma told me if she hadn't loved him so much, she would have shot him that night. My grandparents pretty much lived in poverty after that night. But every time Burt Coty got two nickels to rub together, he got into a poker game or would bet on the racehorses at the Powell County Fair in Deer Lodge.

Leaving the ranch, my grandparents moved into a little rental house next door to my parents. I spent a lot of time with Grandpa Coty. I learned a lot of cool things from him. Well, some things weren't so cool. Gramps was a bare- knuckle boxer and a good one. I was told he was the middleweight Northwest Champion for a few years. He had the lower part of his left ear bitten off in a barroom brawl. His right shoulder had a terrible scar from a horse that bit him while he was trying to break it. He killed that horse by clobbering it with a Quirt. Burt Coty was scary tough. I'm sure the owner of the horse expected to get it back alive.

Much to my mom's chagrin, he taught me how to box and also how to fight to win when I was seven years old. I was told never to start a fight, but never to back away from one, either. Over the years, that advice cost me many black eyes, broken noses, chipped teeth, and a great deal of bleeding.

Gramps wasn't any better at betting on the nags that came to the County Fair to gallop around the track. He would hang around the jockeys so he could gather some "inside intel" on which horse was going to win. Obviously, the little buggers lied to him or didn't have a clue because he rarely, if ever, won anything.

He loved to go fishing, but was the worst fisherman in the world. If he didn't get a bite in twenty seconds or less, he would move to a different spot. He covered a lot of ground, but rarely caught anything. One morning, I asked him to go fishing with me. I told him we should try to fish in a tiny stream called Mullen Creek. It was only about a foot or two deep and three or four feet wide. He wasn't really excited about catching anything in this tiny creek, but he took me there anyway. We walked about fifty yards past the gate leading into the meadow. We put worms on our hooks and lowered the bait into the little slow-moving stream. I watched Gramps as he bobbed his bait up and down. Suddenly, he let out a yell. He had a fish on that was speeding downstream taking all the line out of his reel. He shouted, "What the hell?" and started chasing his fish trying to catch up to it. Finally, the fish tuckered out and Gramps lifted a three-pound rainbow out of the water. In his entire life, he never caught a fish that was more than ten inches long. He thought he had suddenly become a great fisherman. I didn't have the heart to tell him that the week before, there was a fishing derby held at this little stream and these were planted fish. Burt Cody went home with the biggest fish he had ever caught. My mom, dad and brother were sworn to secrecy, and never let him know about the derby.

As previously mentioned, Gramps started every day off by drinking a water glass full of Seagram Seven whiskey with some sugar in it. He thought it was a cure-all for all illnesses. I dreaded getting sick with a cold or the flu because if Gramps caught wind of my sickness, over to our house he would come with whisky and sugar in hand. I begged my mother to lock him out, but she always caved in and let him in. When I had a cold, it wasn't too bad, but the flu was a whole different matter. After a swallow, I would race to the bathroom and puke my guts out. Grandpa would then try to convince me that I was now well on my way to recovery. To this day, I'm not sure which was worse – his remedy or the flu.

My grandfather was in his eighties when he ran the Montana State Prison pig farm located four miles west of Deer Lodge along the Clark Fork River. He was in charge of about 25 so-called trustees. Trustees were mostly check forgers, petty thieves, and small-time robbers, but they weren't murderers or rapists.

I loved going out to the pig farm to stay with Grandma and Grandpa. I had the run of the place. You're probably thinking what's a little boy doing being around a bunch of convicts? I found out, when I was older, that Grandpa Burt met with all the convicts. He told them in no uncertain terms that if any one of them touched me, he would shoot and kill the con that did it and then shoot all the rest of them one by one. There was no question that they believed Grandpa would do just that.

I was about eight when I started going out to the farm to stay with my grandparents. One of the things I really enjoyed was riding a big old grey mare named "Buttermilk." Her top speed was about five miles per hour. To get to ride Buttermilk, I had to cut across a huge pig pen that housed 20 to 30 pigs. To an eight-year-old, they looked as big as elephants. I was sure I would slip and fall into the pen and be eaten alive within minutes. I was scared to death of the mean-looking hogs that were wallowing around in slop. I wanted to ride Buttermilk so much that I was willing to risk my life to do it.

When the old cook, whose name was Cookie, surprise, knew I was going to be staying at the farm, he would always bake a chocolate cake for me. I frequently ate lunch with the convicts.

The farm had a huge brick storage building that housed a bunch of pigeons. Pigeons are notorious crappers and were on the most wanted list to be exterminated. One of the cons asked me if I would like to shoot at the pigeons. "Boy, would I!" About two days later, he gave me a really nice slingshot. I spent hours and hours practicing and shooting at pigeons. If it was small, had feathers or fur, I shot at it. In the process, a few windows were broken.

As I got older, another con made me a bow and some arrows. He was an Indian. Sadly, a lot of Indians were in the Pen. I thought they were nicer than the white guys. I also received a wallet and a horsehair belt.

There were a lot of whitetail deer that lived along the river and in the gullies that were just above the Clark Fork. One of the cons asked my grandpa if he could go hunting for a deer. "Sure, you can," Grandpa said. All would have ended well if the con only used a slingshot or a bow and arrow to go hunting. Instead, Gramps loaned him his thirty-thirty to improve his chances of success. He didn't loan the gun out just once, but three times. Cons have an uncanny way of communicating with their pals in the big house (the main penitentiary).

The warden heard the rumors and called my grandpa on the carpet. He probably could have asked for mercy and kept his job. Maybe! But no, Grandpa told the Warden, who was one strict S.O.B., that he trusted the cons more than he trusted him. It wasn't the first time Grandpa got fired, but it would be his last time. He was somewhere around eighty-eight years old.

Even in his late nineties, Burt Coty would drive his old red Ford pickup down the center of Milwaukee Avenue to get to the Corner Bar where he would no doubt lose a little money playing penny ante poker. Just about everyone in Deer Lodge knew about Grandpa's driving habits, so they just pulled over to the curb and let him pass by. The old bird just couldn't stop playing poker.

We're not sure just how old Gramps was when he died because he either hid or destroyed his birth certificate so he could find work well into his eighties. We guessed he was about one hundred years old when he passed away.

Gramps fell and broke his hip and had to be put into the hospital. He told the doctor and the nurses that he intended to die and that they were wasting their time trying to feed him intravenously. They would put the feeding tube in his arm and as soon as they would leave, he would pull it out. He called all of his immediate family in to explain why he now had to die.

He told me that he couldn't think of any more jokes to tell and that Grandma was in too much pain with her rheumatoid arthritis that she also needed to die. He said that once he was gone, Grandma would soon follow him and that then they could be together again. Grandma pretty much starved herself and died not long after Grandpa. Try as I might, I just couldn't bring myself to go to my dear old friend's funeral. Instead, I talked my mom into driving me out to Mullen Creek so I could put some flowers by the spot where Burt Coty caught the biggest fish of his life.

CHAPTER 5

Playing the Cons

At age sixteen, I was pitching hardball for our American Legion baseball team. At the time, I was going inside the prison to pitch fastpitch softball against the prison team with some of my older friends. There were two distinct sections of the prison. The inside housed the lifers, hard core murders, rapists, assaulters and one guy who ate a psychologist. I'm not kidding. There were about seven hundred of them. The field was totally surrounded by the twenty-foot-high prison walls. Usually, there were about four to five hundred of the insiders watching the game.

I was so little that almost all of them would root for me. They would let me know that they were betting smokes that our team would beat the inmates. I also got a lot of tips, such as "the fat ass catcher can't hit an inside pitch." Another time, one of them told me: "If you bean the shortstop, I'll give you a buck." I considered doing it but just didn't think it was worth it.

During my junior year in high school, the famous prison riot occurred on April 16, 1959, which drew national attention. A bunch of cons rioted and took over the prison. They killed some guards, including the Deputy Warden whose name was Roth. His son was a friend and classmate of mine.

A lot of the ringleader convicts were lifers and had nothing to lose. To encourage the warden to meet their demands, they had about sixteen guards strapped to tilted chairs with ropes tied around their necks. By pulling a release rope, all of the guards would fall over a wall and be hanged.

I used to hang out at the 4Bs restaurant, which was directly across the street from the territorial prison. From there, we had a bird's-eye view of the prison. After staring at the walls for a while, we gave up on seeing any of the action.

The day after we gave up watching, around midnight, all hell broke loose. The National Guard was called in to help end the riots. A guardsman aimed a bazooka at the tower where the guards were being held. I found out a few years ago from a friend of the Guardsman who fired the bazooka that the first shot sailed over the tower and landed in an empty field behind the prison. That was never reported in any newspaper or magazine article. The second shot was a bullseye. It blasted into the upper corner of the tower. The concussion of the blast stunned and confused the inmates. One of the ringleaders shot himself and the others gave up quickly. None of the guards lost their lives by being hanged. Thank the good Lord, it was nothing short of a miracle. The riot put Deer Lodge on the map for a short time. A few years later, a new prison was built about three miles west of town. It was named in honor of my friend's dad who lost his life during the riot. Somehow, the riot didn't stop me from going into the prison to play softball. It should have.

The prison riot made national news, and that summer, Montana was in the news again. Somehow, I was selected to go to Boys' State by the Elks' Club in Deer Lodge. To be selected, you had to have strong leadership qualities, be a good student and citizen. Apparently, the Elks weren't aware of my many misdeeds. Boys' State was held at Western Montana College, located in Dillon. We checked in on Friday, August 16th, and spent most of Saturday in workshops. The workshop speakers mentioned several times that we were the future leaders of Montana. I started to think there might be hope for me.

Four of us were staying on the 4th floor of the dorm. It was a long day, so we all went to sleep around 11:00 p.m. I had just fallen asleep when I woke up thinking someone was shaking my bed. It was hopping all over the place. I looked down at the floor and saw a big crack running across it. We opened the shaking door and headed for the back marble stairs, taking us out of the shaking building. A huge crack was opening up on the main floor. We got out! You probably guessed that, or I wouldn't be writing this book.

The earthquake registered 7.9 on the Richter Scale. It created a massive landslide of about 80 million tons of rock. It's almost unbelievable that the slide moved at 100 MPH. It created Quake Lake, which is six miles long and 160 feet deep. Twenty-eight people died in the rockslide. Where we were staying was about 35 miles from the epicenter of the quake, as the crow flies.

Over the years, I probably went into the prison to play softball fifty or more times. Years later, some of my fastpitch buddies decided that we should get together one more time to play the inmates. We were now all in our thirties. I looked over who was playing for the inmates, and I didn't like what I saw. In right field was a big ex-Montana State football player who raped and dragged under his car a beautiful young lady who was a sweetheart of Sigma Chi, my fraternity. He killed her by dragging her to death. I had an intense hatred for him. In centerfield was an even bigger thug who was in for jamming a screwdriver through the heads of an elderly couple outside a bar in a small town in central Montana. The catcher was bald, missing most of his teeth and was truly butt-ugly. I noticed that none of the cons would sit next to him. I asked the Athletic Director what he did to get into prison. "He's the worst of the worst, and you don't want to know what he did, believe me!" Thank the good lord that the guy who ate the psychologist didn't like playing softball.

The game was going pretty well until the third inning when I was playing third base and a con slid into the bag head-first. I didn't mean to tag him in the head, mostly on his jaw. Crap, he was really woozy and had a hard time standing up. A few of the cons next to the wall had a few choice comments to make. I remember one of them accused me of having sex with some goats. Other comments were made that were not so complimentary.

The next inning, a con, while going into second base, went in really high and spiked our shortstop in the thigh. It was obviously intentional. Our shortstop told me between innings that: "If another con comes in high, I am going to aim at his head to get him to slide on the ground." You know what's coming, two innings later, another con came flying into second, really high, trying to spike our short stop. As promised, our shortstop, who had a good arm, threw at the con's head, catching him at the top of his forehead. He didn't knock him out, but it was damn close.

I turned and saw a bunch of cons standing up and moving toward us. I grabbed a bat, thinking I might as well go down swinging. Our whole team ran to our sideline, some picking up bats for defense.

About that time, when I thought I might be beaten to death, I saw some guards on the wall above us raise their machine guns, pointing them at the oncoming mass of inmates and us. Knowing most of the guards, I just knew that they would shoot some of us as well as a bunch of convicts. Then, I heard the Athletic Director scream for us to get into line. We quickly got into line and were marched across the field to the nearest exit door. Once we were all safely behind the closed steel door, we suddenly became really brave. Things were said. For example, "Lucky cons, we would have kicked their asses." Yeah, right. We all knew we were lucky to get out of there in one piece. We all agreed that we would never return, and we never did.

CHAPTER 6

Powell County High School: Pigs, Cows, Horses & Sheep

Martha Hole was one of my classmates in high school. She was a nice, quiet young lady who lived on the westside of town. Her father's name was Alfred. When I first noticed their mailbox, I broke out laughing. As God is my witness, and big as life, it said "A. HOLE" in big black letters. Good old Alfred either didn't care or was unaware of what a lot of us demented people knew what A-hole stood for.

Sometimes, we got bored living in what we fondly called Dead Lodge. To combat the boredom, some of my friends, after a lot of thought and preparation, managed to get a fairly large cow up to the third floor of our high school. A cow can be moved on level ground without too much difficulty, but getting one up these slippery marble floors is a completely different matter. Of course, the cow chose not to use the restrooms available. I don't even want to get into how hard it must be to borrow a cow to parade around your high school. I'm taking that information with me to my grave or to the fire box.

Another young lady in my class was Margaret Hollowpeter. We had a goofy student teacher, who, reading roll for the first time in English class, tried to change her name to Halopeter. Ms. Hollowpeter quickly informed him its "Hollowpeter!" I thought it was pretty darn cool that we had Alfred Hole and Margaret Hollowpeter in our little town.

My favorite class was beginning typing, which was taught by our head football coach. He was a big burly man, who had played some professional football in Canada. He would take attendance and then say: "OK guys, turn to page 20 and start typing." Then he would sit down in his big old swivel chair, turn his back to us, put his feet up on a chair, lean back and go to sleep. To my credit, I typed away for two days. On the third day, it occurred to me that I could leave class for at least a half hour and then come back for the last ten minutes of class. That gave me enough time to dash over to a little neighborhood grocery store, which was close to the high school, and get a snack. Needless to say, I'm a hunt-and-peck typist to this day.

My second favorite class was Algebra One taught by a very old man who had poor eyesight and couldn't hear thunder. I seized on the opportunity to exit the class without being noticed. Sometimes, I would sneak out and go to the boy's bathroom for a little smoke. I thought, what the heck, I was raised in the back of a smoky bowling alley, so a few puffs on a Lucky Strike wouldn't do too much damage to me other than stunt my growth. No one mentioned lung cancer at that time.

Speaking of smoking, I did try out for the track team my freshman year. I was too little to do anything other than run. I tried out for the mile. During the first time-trial, fast Freddy Humpreville, also known as the bun humper, (we had no idea why we called him that), had lapped me before I had finished my second lap. As I was chugging along, I slowly passed by the head track coach, who yelled: "Do you want to be a manager?" I took one more step, made a right turn and walked back to our locker room. I turned in my gear. Thus ended a very, very brief and unspectacular track career.

Other than baseball, (I could throw a curve ball when I was seven years old), football was my favorite sport. My senior year, I was all of five feet six inches tall and weighed a whopping one hundred and forty-six pounds. I liked football so much that I quit smoking during football season. Also, I didn't drink even one beer. That's dedication!

Because of injuries and getting caught drinking, most of the seniors didn't get to play football. I was left with a bunch of juniors and sophomores, who had little or no ability to play football. Excuse my language, but they were the shits. One of the few seniors who kind of played, hated contact so he became a kicking specialist. Because we rarely scored, he got to kick only twice. He damn near whiffed on his first attempt, the ball traveling about five feet in the air. His second attempt he made better contact and kicked the ball at a perfect trajectory to hit me in the butt. To his defense, I did center the ball a little bit too high, but come on!

I know you're going to be shocked, but by the time our last game came around, we were winless. Shoot, we were almost scoreless. Our last game was against a very small school located a little west of us, the Stevensville Yellowjackets. We found out that their coach tried to forfeit the game because most of their team was out sick with the flu. But our coach, being the cunning rascal he was, smelled a win and insisted they show up. Well, let me tell you, we socked it to the sick little buggers, beating them by a touchdown.

Speaking of breaking training rules, my senior year we had a pretty good basketball team. We were favored to win the district tournament. When we went on road trips, our coaches took turns driving the bus. They smoked cigarettes while doing so. When they lit up in front of the bus, we lit up in the back of the bus. After a while, you couldn't see three feet ahead of you because of the smoke. When we got to our motel rooms, on overnight trips, we would gather into one room, until the coaches told us it was time to go to the gym. Our smoking room looked like it had been set on fire. We were winning, so we knew we wouldn't be kicked off the team.

After we won our last conference game, we all met at our favorite watering hole about two miles north of town at Cottonwood Creek for a kegger. Being the disciplined jocks we were, we decided to be good and only drink beer until midnight. We would then go to town and eat some burgers at the 4B's café. Everything was OK, until the manager got the bright idea that it would be great fun to take a little drive in the Highway Patrolman's car that was parked in front of the 4B's. In those days, a lot of folks left their keys in their cars. He didn't get very far and was caught by the local police. Our beloved manager, to save his sorry butt, caved in and told the authorities the names of all of us who were at the kegger.

On Monday morning, we were called into the principal's office and were told we were kicked off the team and as further punishment, we had to attend the tournament game Deer Lodge played in, as spectators. I didn't give a hoot about upsetting our coaches, but for the rest of my life, I felt horrible for badly upsetting my parents.

While setting pins, I met Jackie Jennings, who was a year older than I was. Jackie was a nice-looking guy and was very strong. I was afraid not to be his friend because I just knew he was certifiably nuts. One day, I was walking downtown when Jackie pulled over in a huge car he either stole or took from his parents. I think it was a big old Oldsmobile. He said, "get in." I was afraid to say no. I should have run. He drove me out of town about five miles where there is an overpass bridge. Jackie floor-boarded the Olds and the last time I looked, it was going over a hundred miles an hour. I jumped into the backseat, thinking I had a better chance of not dying. How he made it over the bridge without killing us, I'll never know. Dreading what might happen next, I told Jackie that I had to take a leak. It was a wonder I didn't already poop my pants. I got out of the car, walked down into the barrow pit and then jumped over a barbed wire fence and ran like I was possessed toward the frontage road that could take me back to Deer Lodge. I decided I would rather have Jackie beat the snot out of me than die in a car crash.

Several seniors decided it would be great fun to initiate Jackie during the first week of high school. Whatever they did to him, made him really ticked off. Somehow Jackie managed to find an alphabetical list of all the senior boys. He took the list and pasted it on the bulletin board in the school cafeteria. Underneath the list, he wrote the following note: "Senior boys. I will fight every one of you starting with the A's. Anderson, you're first. Meet me at noon tomorrow behind the Vo-Ag building." During the weeks following his challenge, Jackie won all of his fights until he got down to the H's. Then, he met his match when Jim Heide showed up. Heide was the first guy I'd met that looked like he was on steroids. He had massive arms and knew how to box. Jackie finally bit the dust.

Shortly after Jackie got tuned up, he dropped out of school. Many years later, I was told that he ran over and killed a highway patrolman. He was sentenced to death row. I'm sure glad he liked me most of the time.

About the middle of my sophomore year, the lady who lived next door to us knocked on our door and was in a panic. She said the night before, while she was in her bathroom getting ready to go to bed, she saw a man staring at her through the bathroom window. She didn't know who he was. Her husband was away on a business trip. She asked my parents if I could stay in her basement until her husband got home. This could be fun … or not. What if he showed up when I was there? She said he was really tall and I'm really short.

In the basement, I could see the window well where the peeping tom had to stand to peep thru the bathroom window. The first night seemed to last forever. I finally dozed off about one in the morning. I woke up at two and went home to sleep in my own bed. I had my doubts about being a peeper catcher. Even though I had reservations, I went over for a second night of peeper duty. After about an hour, I was listening to some music on the radio and looking at the window hoping to see some legs. I heard a sound like gravel crunching, yikes! I was looking at legs. I thought my heart was going to explode. I ran upstairs and threw the backdoor open. I jumped down the back steps and landed on the ground about ten feet from the peeper. I yelled at the top of my lungs: "Don't move." Damn, he was really, really tall. For an instant, I thought I just caught Ichabod Crane. Peeper was skinny and dressed in all black. He took off running thru my folks' backyard and started up dad's flower garden steps. That's where I tackled him, all 125 pounds of me. Peeper was well over six feet tall and if he wanted to, could have probably beat the bejesus out of me. To my surprise, he started crying and was shaking like a leaf. When I finally saw his face, I couldn't believe my eyes. He was a neighbor who lived about two blocks from us. The old bugger was at mass every Sunday with his family. I went to school with two of his kids.

He pleaded with me not to tell my dad what he had been doing. He respected my father and didn't want him to know he was 'The Peeper'. "Please don't tell your father! I promise I will never ever look into anyone's window, so help me God." He was sobbing so hard, I believed him. I told him I had to tell my dad, but I would ask him not to tell anyone else and he never did. That weekend, the lady next door took me to Dairy Queen and bought me a hot fudge sundae. Wow! She also gave me twenty bucks. Maybe I just found a cool way to earn a few bucks. Unfortunately, or fortunately, there weren't enough peeping toms in Deer Lodge to make it worthwhile. Also, I couldn't properly advertise my peeper-catching skills. Finally, some of us should have apologized to the slightly goofy neighbor across the street who owned a toy store. We all thought HE was the peeper. We never told him what we thought. Probably a good decision.

My dad would always come home to eat dinner between 5:45 P.M. and 6:30 P.M., then go back to the bowling alley to start the seven o'clock shift. When dad was home to eat, someone was breaking into the side door to the bowling alley and stealing money out of the cash register. It happened twice in two weeks. I guess because I did such a good job catching peeper, my dad asked me if I would walk down to the bowling alley around five and then stay there when he went home to eat. The thief wouldn't know I was there and then I could nab them when they broke in. I asked Dad: "What if it's a really big guy, what should I do?" His response: "You're really fast – just see who it is and run like hell out the back door." My second question: "Why me? Why not my older brother?" Dad's answer: "He's afraid, and he said you're tougher than he is." My thought – "And, he's smarter too.'"

Every day for three days, I stayed hidden in the bowling alley. Nothing happened except I ate a bunch of candy bars. On the fourth day around six, I heard a noise by the side door. Someone breaking into the bowling alley. Talk about an adrenaline rush. After a cracking noise, the side door slowly opened. I crouched down behind the front counter waiting to see who it was. To my delight, it was Jerry McComber, one of my classmates who used to set pins for my dad. I sprung out from behind the counter and told him not to run because you know I can outrun you. He was had. I called my dad and told him I caught the thief. Poor old Jerry had the longest wait of his life. Nobody but nobody wanted to be on the wrong end of my father's wrath. I'm pretty sure Jerry peed his pants. Waiting for Dad to show up was already a lot of punishment. He had to pay back the money he stole and pay for the damage to the door. Jerry never came near me again.

CHAPTER 7

Flying Tires and Bucking Cars

During the summer of my junior year in high school, my dad was going to be out of town on a business trip for two weeks. The last thing he told me was: "Do not drive our four-wheel-drive Jeep station wagon anywhere!"

Oftentimes during my high school years, my mind seemed to go on vacation. The following was one of those times. I called four of my buddies to see if they wanted to go up to Rock Creek Lake in Dad's Jeep for a little party. Of course, they all wanted in on the fun. We knew an older guy who, for a few extra bucks, would buy us beer. We loaded up with lots of beer and stuff to eat and took off for the lake.

Rock Creek Lake was located about ten miles west of Deer Lodge. You got there on a rough, rocky road. About halfway there, after I had already downed a couple of Great Falls Select beers, we got to a steep gully called Mullen Gulch. Being slightly impaired, I drove down at a nice rate of speed, but I underestimated how sharp the turn was at the bottom of the hill. Pop's pride and joy Jeep went airborne and then slammed into a huge boulder. Smacko – we hit so hard that the left front tire shot up into the air landing a long way away. The force of the collision knocked the glass out of the rearview mirror, and it went into the forehead of Jack the Quack Kendrick. Blood streamed down into his eyes. He jumped out of the Jeep and ran around in circles yelling, "I'm blind!" I managed to catch him and wipe the blood out of his eyes. It took quite a while to convince him he could see again.

Surveying the situation and seeing that the front tire was shot and the rim was really bent, we decided the only logical thing to do was to continue driving to the lake. It was slow going driving on a tireless bent rim. I could only manage three or four miles an hour. The old Jeep wanted to veer to the left. A couple of beers later, we arrived at the campground. We quickly set up camp and then proceeded to drink our fool heads off. It was really cold that night, but we had a huge bonfire and sleeping bags.

I tried to convince my bloody-forehead buddy that he was trying to sleep too close to the fire. He wasn't having any of my advice. About an hour or so after we went to sleep, we were suddenly awakened to a blood-curdling scream. Jack's sleeping bag was on fire. Being really close to the lake, it was easy to pour too much water on him. One of our lot poured beer on Jack. What a waste of beer. Jack was lucky to just get singed a little bit.

The next morning, the drive back to Deer Lodge seemed to take forever. What seemed like more than forever was the day of reckoning when my father was due home in five days. I would be lucky if he just skinned me alive. Finally, he drove into our driveway. I went outside to meet him even before he could get out of the car. "Dad, I took the Jeep to Rock Creek Lake with some buddies, and I drove too fast down Mullen Gulch and missed the turn and almost rolled the Jeep." I left out the beer part and the party at the lake. "What's so bad is that I disobeyed you and drove the Jeep." "I'll pay for fixing it and if you want to smack me, go ahead, I deserve it." All Dad said was, "you will pay for it and for six months you won't be riding or driving anywhere." You can walk, run or ride your bike to work. Do you want to go backpacking up to Elbow Lake next weekend?" Holy Smokes, did I ever luck out or what?

You're probably thinking that I was nothing but a little drunk during my high school years. For one thing, I never drank during football season. For another, I couldn't drink even a swallow of beer for months without puking. Here's what happened. My sophomore year, I was walking home from downtown on the afternoon of New Year's Eve. On the way home, I stopped by a friend's house to see what he was doing. It wasn't long before he said, "Hey, Gordy, Dad's got a bunch of Lucky Larger in the fridge – you want one?" I said "sure," and things went downhill from there. We each downed three beers. Then, the next bright idea: "Hey, let's see what old pop has in his liquor cabinet. This blackberry brandy looks good. Want some?" I thought, why not, after all its New Year's Eve afternoon. I tossed down four or five shots and told my friend that I had better be on my way. I staggered my way home, which was about eight blocks away. I managed to get inside in time to toss my cookies in the bathroom. I told Mom that I didn't feel very well and was going upstairs to my bedroom. I was so sick. When Dad came home from work, he came upstairs to check on me. He arrived just in time for me to throw up on his shoes. Nice! He didn't say a word, which really made me nervous. I had the dry heaves for three days. I deserved all seventy-two hours of it. There was some good that came from my indiscretion. For well over a year, I couldn't even smell a beer, let alone drink one. To this day, I know that I couldn't even open a bottle of blackberry brandy. Sadly, I was a persistent little cuss, so I started taking a little sip of beer without barfing. Little by little, the sips turned into being able to drink a full beer.

Just one more drinking story, OK? During the summer, I had a really great job putting ice into the end compartments on the railroad car. The railroad cars came from Washington State, carrying loads of potatoes. This was before there were refrigerated cars. There would be two or three railroad cars filled with solid blocks of ice. Our job was to break off big chunks of ice and put them on a platform that was about twenty feet off the ground. Then, we would wait about six or seven hours for the train to come in. They were always late, so we always got overtime. Once the train came in, we would get up on the platform in a hurry and push the blocks of ice into the compartments. It took about thirty minutes to get the job done.

So, most of the time, we had six or seven hours to kill. A lot of times, we just slept on mattresses that we hauled into a warming shed. But, sometimes, we would go downtown to get a bite to eat. No problem until one night, when my partner, Bats Luce, suggested that we go to Landen's Bar and toss down a few drinks. After consuming one too many, Bats, in his inebriated state, said: "I know that I can drive the three-wheeled rodeo car that was parked behind the bar." A rodeo car is steered by using foot pedals. If you push both pedals down, it will buck up into the air and spin around. It takes some practice and skill to drive one. Bats assigned me to be co-pilot. We convinced six drunken friends to push us to get the bucking spinner started.

It did start and we started lurching, bucking and spinning down the alley. Actually, Bats was doing a remarkable job of keeping the car between the sidewalks. We made it one block over to Main Street. We were getting a lot of laughs from onlookers. Everything seemed to be really funny until the Deputy Sheriff, who luckily was a good friend of ours, pulled up alongside of us and said: "You're going to jail unless you get that damn thing back to the bar." All righty then, we obliged and made a left turn and headed back to the bar by way of Second Street. All was going swimmingly until a little old lady, wouldn't you know it, was driving toward us. Bats, thinking he might hit her, panicked, and took evasive action. He slammed both foot pedals down, the Rodeo Car jumped up, spun around and went over the curb and onto the splendid courthouse lawn. We smashed through a flower garden, and broke three water spigots. It looked like little geysers going off behind us. Worst of all, we were rapidly heading toward the front steps of the Courthouse. Bats jammed both pedals down again and the car bucked straight up and landed in a huge fir tree. With a lot of luck, and not much skill, we somehow backed out of the tree.

Landers Bar was just across the street from the courthouse, so we got the car back to the bar without killing ourselves or someone else. We went into the bar to confess. The owner of the car and the bar was waiting for us. Bats said: "We took it and hardly did any damage to the town, but man did we have a good time." The owner observed, "I'll just bet you did. Now, get the hell out of here and go back to work!"

Going back to work was without incident except for the fire hose we ran over. Just our luck, they had a fire close to our work site. We never figured out why we didn't get into hot water for going over that hose.

After finishing up our work at the icehouse, we decided to eat breakfast at the 4B's café. We just started chowing down when in comes our Deputy Sheriff friend who said, "I've been looking all over for you dorks. There is a warrant out for your arrest. Get your sorry butts down to the Sheriff's office now!"

The Sheriff's office was located immediately behind the Courthouse. Passing by and seeing the damage we caused, it wasn't hard to figure out that this one is going to cost us a bunch. The Sheriff was more than willing to give us a tour of the Courthouse flower beds, busted water spigots, and a fir tree with several broken branches. He proceeded to question our maturity and our common sense. "And to think you're a teacher, Bats, and Gordon, you're going to be a teacher. I wonder what the kids are going to be in for. You have to pay for all the damages and that's all because I don't know what else I can charge you with." Wow, did we luck out. It could have been car theft, reckless driving, driving under the influence, and so on. We had to promise never to do anything this stupid again. To this day, I'm not sure I've ever had a better time!

CHAPTER 8

So I Went to College …

When I wasn't spending my summers doing Marine Corps stuff, I decided that college might be the way to go. I had no clue what career I wanted to pursue. I knew I didn't want to run a bowling alley, as I had enough of that growing up. Also, I wanted to play some more football after my miserable high school experience. So being a Catholic, I sent a letter to the head football coach at Carroll College, a NAIA school in Helena, Montana, only fifty miles from Deer Lodge. The letter described by physical attributes. I lied.

I told the coach I was 5 feet 11 inches and weighed 195 pounds. When I showed up at camp, I was actually 5 feet 7 inches and 165 pounds, but I was still growing, just not fast enough. Coach John looked me over and asked me when my big brother was going to show up to play football. I quickly let him know I was still growing and that it runs in the family and that I might end up really big. He said:

"You must be a running back?" "Nope, I'm a middle linebacker and a center." His response: "You've got to be kidding me! Well, good luck, you're going to need it."

It was really hot that fall and we had to practice three times a day – six in the morning, noon and four in the afternoon. At the end of "three-a-days," I weighed a whopping one hundred fifty-seven pounds. I thought my best shot was playing center. There were seven other guys trying out for center and a veteran we knew was really good and couldn't be beat out. The smallest of the seven was about six feet and around two hundred pounds and was a little faster than I was. I just dug in and tried my hardest, figuring any day, my name was sure to appear on the cut list. The last thirty-three players got a scholarship of three hundred dollars. What a deal!

A last and final scrimmage was scheduled before the final cut was made. They finally put me in at center. I was lined up against a senior who had been in the Marine Corps for eight years. He was bald and was missing several teeth. He was about six feet tall and weighed two hundred fifty pounds. He was a unanimous all-conference nose guard. He was known as the conference bad-ass and probably set a record for collecting the most unsportsmanlike penalties. I knew I had no chance of blocking him if I went straight at him. I dove at his feet hoping he would trip over me. Apparently that little move made him angry. He got up, pushed my head into the ground and then stepped on my hand, grinding his steel spikes. If you haven't had a two hundred fifty-pound nose guard step on your hand, I can tell you it really hurts. I told him not to do it again or I would kick his ass (like that was going to happen). He said: "I'll do it again if you don't block like a man."

I'm thinking that I'm going to get cut anyway, so I snapped the ball and dove at his ankles again. He jumped up and stomped on my hand. I lost my temper and thought I might as well go down in flames. I grabbed his face mask, lifted it up as much as I could and slugged him in the face. Suddenly, I was airborne. He slammed me into the ground. Next, he ripped my helmet off and proceeded to pummel me until he got tired of watching me bleed. The coaches never stopped fights between the players. Nice.

I managed to get on my feet and slowly walked to our dressing room, bleeding all over the place. I gathered up all of my gear to turn it into the equipment manager. The equipment guy said, "Hey, maybe you ought to check the cut list before you turn in your gear." I'm thinking it's a waste of time, but I will go check it just to make him happy. I couldn't find my name on the list. The coaches must have made a mistake.

I went to see Coach Hundhausen to see why I wasn't on the list. "I can't cut you!" "Why not?" "Your friend that just beat the crap out of you said if I cut you then I had to cut him too. As you know, he's not going to be cut, so you just made the cut."

I went back to the locker room and found my new nose guard buddy. I said thanks. He glared at me and said if I didn't block him like a man, he would give me a worse beating. ", Oh-key-do-key, you can run over me for the rest of the season." So, I sort of made the team and received a whopping $300 scholarship that was given to the top 33 players.

I really looked forward to going on the road for an away game. Our first road game was in Utah to play Westminster. We always rode to away games in a bus. We didn't fly anywhere. We arrived in Salt Lake City Friday afternoon, the day before our Saturday game.

Getting off the bus, I was anxious to see who my roommate was going to be, hoping it was one of my freshman buddies. It wasn't. Instead, it was our all-conference defensive end, a senior who had a reputation for being a little bit nuts. He played without any regard for the welfare of his body. He was a punt blocking machine. I just had to ask Coach why I was assigned a room with a senior, especially a crazy one. "Well, he said, I put you with him because you're a little bit goofy too, so you two are already messed up, so you can't do too much damage to each other. If I put you guys with other players, you could mess them up."

He got to the room before me and before I could say anything, he asked me: "Do you smoke?" I told him I was raised in the back of a bowling alley and inhaled a ton of second-hand smoke. "Go over and open up the window and let's have one." I guess our coach knew what he was doing. The next day my goofy roommate blocked two punts with his face.

If you were a freshman or sophomore male student at Carroll College, you were required to live in an old four-story dorm built out of big rocks. It, the dorm, reminded me of the prison in my hometown. The priests ran the dorm with an iron fist, much like prison wardens. You could study until 10 and then you were locked in your room and lights had to be turned off. A priest would come around and check each room to make sure we were in bed and, heaven forbid, not studying. After the poor priest who was on check-in duty left, sometimes we would stuff towels into the crack at the bottom of our door so we could play cards or on very rare occasions, study.

I was joined in pursuing an education, or at least pretending to, by three of my friends from Deer Lodge. My best friend in high school, Doug Rives, agreed to be my roommate. Doug and I shared some similar interests. One of the interests was not studying unless absolutely necessary. Another was to see who could sleep in the longest. After a year, Doug transferred to the University of Montana and became an excellent student. Doug went on to become a very successful entrepreneur. I suspect getting away from me was a very good thing for Doug's success. The other two Deer Lodge guys were Bob Daniels and John Hanson. Both Bob and John were really smart, and both had basketball scholarships. Doug and I both admired their dedication to their studies and to their athletic careers. We gave them a lot of "that-a-boy's" and "go-get-em's."

Bob Daniels owned an enormous '54 Chrysler that looked like a tug boat. Every now and then, being bored with studying, we decided to stuff our beds, to make them look like we were in them sleeping, and sneak out after the priest checked us in for the night. John Hanson used a coconut and a stocking cap over it to fool the check-in priest. It worked. Either that or the priest laughed himself silly and let us off the hook. Off we would go to Deer Lodge to arrive at Dad's bowling alley. I had a key, so we were good to go. We would bowl until about four in the morning and then head back to Carroll. We would drink a gallon of coffee and show up at our eight o'clock classes bleary-eyed. Is it any wonder I barely managed a C average my freshman year?

When my dad turned ninety, I confessed to him about our early morning bowling escapades. His only response was: "I always knew you guys were a bunch of knot-heads." He couldn't get too mad at me because on weekends, when I wasn't playing football, I used to hitchhike to Deer Lodge to help him run the bowling alley. If I got down to Helena's Main Street by 8 A.M., I could get a ride to Deer Lodge with the Eddy's Bakery delivery guy. Of course, it took quite a bit of time because he had to make about twenty stops. I had to take my chances hitchhiking back on Sunday night.

I didn't have a clue about what I wanted to do for a living or what kind of career to pursue. My mom thought I would make a great priest. Obviously, my mom was an extremely forgiving person. To make her happy, I gave it a five-day shot. My line coach, Joe Pat Sullivan, talked me into staying at a special dorm for five days to pray and see if I got the "calling." I realized the first day that it wasn't going to work. I kept eyeballing the co-eds as they walked by going to class. I admit that I even had such bad thoughts like: "Boy, I think she would be fun to bang!" I went back to the regular dorms after two days. Mom was happy that I tried at least.

My freshman year was sort of a bust. I did the bare minimum of studying, barely getting a C average. One bright spot, however, was that I was a member of the Carroll College bowling team that won the national NAIA bowling tournament. Three of the five guys on the team had dads who ran bowling alleys. We should have been good!

My brother was attending Montana State University and he sent me a nice letter saying that he wanted me to transfer to MSU. It sounded like a good idea, so off I went to Bozeman, Montana. Again, I had to live in a dorm. My first roommate was a friend from Deer Lodge, who was seriously studying to become an architect. On many nights, he would study until two or three in the morning. A lot of times, I would just be arriving home from a night on the town. I drove him crazy.

Because I still was clueless about what I wanted to do career-wise, I took classes that sounded like they would be fun rather than useful. I ended up with five minors before I finally graduated. After two quarters of driving Joe Grover nuts, I moved to another room. My new roommate was on the MSU football team. He was one hell of a player. His name was Willie Finnell. He ended up playing for the Minnesota Vikings. We got along great. He once told me that he thought I had some fairly serious mental problems. To this day, I think he was probably correct. I realized how difficult it was to be a black man going to school in Bozeman, Montana. I'm a lot of things, but being a racist isn't one of them.

My grades were still only average, and I spent little time studying. I got invited to join Sigma Chi fraternity, which was a blessing. I only got in because my brother was a 'Brother'. That sounds funny, doesn't it? More about the Sigs later. Unfortunately, I still wanted to play football, and knowing I had to get bigger, I lifted a lot of weights and ate like a pig. Also, I was still growing taller.

On weekends, I drove to Deer Lodge to help run the bowling alley. I bought a '54 Ford for $450. It barely ran, but I knew just enough about car engines to nurse it along. Good thing I did, because a lot went wrong with the old Ford.

During my sophomore year at MSU, I was on their bowling team. We won the national NCAA tournament. Here's a trivia question for you: Who was the only person to win the NAIA and NCAA national bowling tournaments? Answer: me. A better question might be, "who cares?"

My first year of being a Sigma Chi, I met a Red Lodge cowboy named Kurt Zook. Kurt was a 6'3", raw-boned left-hander who was really smart and super competitive. Because I was raised in a bowling alley, I was a pretty good barroom athlete. I could shoot pool, bowl and arm wrestle really well. Kurt was a great arm wrestler. We found out that there was some money to be made at a cowboy bar in Belgrade, Montana, which was about ten miles south of Bozeman. Kurt, being left-handed, took on the lefties and I would do the honors for anyone who wanted to try me right-handed. We put up twenty dollars a match. The first weekend, I made about two hundred dollars. Kurt made about the same.

The next Saturday night, I won my first two matches fairly easily. My third match was against a huge cowboy, who was about 6'4" and around 250 pounds. I got the jump on him and slammed his arm down. No sweat. Either his wife or his girlfriend laughed at him for being beaten by a little guy like me. Instantly, I knew I might be in a world of hurt. He stood up and said: "We're going outside and I'm going to get my money's worth." Seeing no way out, I followed him outside. I should have run out the backdoor. I no more than got out the door when John Wayne Jr. picked me up by my neck and sent his huge fist towards my face. I ducked as much as I could. I felt his fist graze the top of my head and heard the plywood door shatter as his fist went through it. It got stuck a little, but he managed to pull his hand back out. His second punch, after he took dead aim, landed on my jaw. In the next minute or two, he had a good time beating me to a pulp. I guess he finally got his money's-worth and he dropped me to the ground in a bloody heap.

I looked at Kurt out of the one eye I could still see out of and said: "Thanks for your help." Kurt said: "Hell, I thought you were going to kick his ass. He isn't all that tough." Really? The Belgrade cowboy heard what Kurt said and called out: "Hey, skinny, you're next!" Watching through my one eye that was still open, I saw Kurt tune him up with ease. All Kurt said was: "I told you he was a wimp." Off I went to the emergency room to get my nose put back in place and to make sure I wouldn't bleed to death. What hurt me the most was I had to fork over $475 to get patched up. Making money arm-wrestling was now out of the question. And you were starting to think I was slow learner!

Even though I had a nice time at MSU, I couldn't get the thought of not playing football out of my banged-up noggin. Now, I was fifty pounds heavier and a whole lot stronger than I was as a freshman and I was almost 5'11". I just knew I could do a lot better and even help the team win.

In late August, I reported to "two-a-days." It sure felt good to tackle someone and not get tea-kettled. (Deer Lodge speak for "run over"). After eight days of practice, I was called into the coach's office. I was sure he was going to tell me what a great job I was doing. Instead, he said: "I have some bad news for you. You have to sit out a year when you transfer from a NCAA school to a NAIA school." My response: "I was told by someone I trusted that I would be eligible to play right away." "Well, whoever told you that was wrong. We looked it up." Coach said: "You're doing really well and if you want to, you can continue practicing with us. It will help you play better next year." I was lower than a snake belly. For two more weeks, I continued to practice. All the players said I was nuts. My heart just wasn't in it and I decided to give up my dream. I always wondered what could have been – probably just more concussions!

Because I was a junior, I could live off campus. My old cowboy friend, Kurt Zook, had graduated in electrical engineering and got a job with Mountain States Telephone in Helena. He called and asked me if I wanted to share an apartment with him. Of course, I said yes. After about a month, I received a call from the pilot of the rodeo car, Bats Luce, saying he needed a place to stay. He had a job working at a local bank in Helena. Sure, we'll find a place for you. He was a longtime friend who was goofy as hell and a whole lot of fun. I found out that Bats, after graduating from college, went to California to strike it rich selling cemetery plots. He had little or no luck doing so. He came back to Montana, depressed and feeling like he was a failure. It didn't help a whole lot that the only space we had left in the apartment was in the boiler room. Bats thought it served him right and it just added to his misery. I knew Bats would bounce back and be his old crazy self.

I finally decided to get serious about college studies and signed up for 24 semester credits in History. I went from hardly ever studying to hardly ever not studying. I did manage to mess around on weekends.

What became difficult was trying to be a student when my two roommates would bring their girlfriends over to fool around. Being respectful, I went into the dungeon, better known as the boiler room, to study.

Kurt and Bats were both highly competitive and good athletes. Not bragging, OK, I'm bragging a little, I was also a pretty fair jock. Kurt said, 'I bet I can throw a softball further than you two wimps!' We went to a football field to see who had the best arm. I threw last. Kurt and Bats went out to argue which of them had thrown the ball the furthest. Meanwhile, I crossed over the end line by about twenty yards and let it rip. The ball sailed over their heads. I raised my hands in the air declaring myself the victor. We always bet six packs. I was on my third beer when my conscience got the best of me. I confessed.

Another really dumb contest was to see who could drink the most water glasses full of vodka without puking. What were we thinking? We weren't. I came in a distant third in that contest.

The school year went along without much that was interesting. However, some of the choices I made right before closing time at a bar weren't the smartest. As an example, I can tell you that I made quite an impression on a young lady whose nickname was Spider Lady because of her physical attributes. Thankfully, she didn't bite me before I departed for home.

Later in the year, I danced with a really hot chick. I was so impressed with her that I promised to show up at her apartment for breakfast the next morning. I even told her I would wash her car. I can be a smooth dude. I was at her doorstep as promised. Surprise. This really stacked chick was about two hundred and fifty pounds on an early morning weigh. She was stacked alright. Just like a haystack. To my credit, I washed her car. I hope the Good Lord noticed. I went home thinking I need to seriously stop drinking around any damsels who might say yes to a date. Thinking back about the breakfast car wash date, I could have pretty happily been married to a very large lady who could really cook and was nice as could be. Being the deplorably shallow person I am, there was no chance.

And so it was back to MSU for my next year. You're probably thinking, when is this guy going to make up his confused mind? Believe me, I was thinking the same thing. I enjoyed my first year at MSU for many of the wrong reasons. Now, I was determined to turn my life around. A good start was the decision to move into the Sigma Chi fraternity house. To stay there, you had to maintain a 3.0 GPA or a B average. Just what I needed.

Every year, a homecoming dance was held at the student union building. About two thousand students attended. One of the main attractions was an arm-wrestling contest that was held midway through the evening. The Sigs wanted me to compete in the middle weight division. All of the fraternities and several independents were in the contest. I nailed my first two opponents easily. Then, I watched two really strong guys wrestle for a long time until finally one prevailed. I doubted that I could beat either one of them. I wrestled the worn-out winner in the final. I beat him to the punch and won. To this day, I believe he would have beaten me if he wasn't so tired.

Now comes the fun part! While I was watching the rest of the matches, one of my fraternity brothers came up to me and said: "Hey, our heavyweight is hurt, do you want to take his place?" "Why not? What's to lose?" I'm not supposed to win anyway, so I jumped into the fray.

I kid you not – my first opponent was a huge man that was an All-Conference Offensive Tackle. He stood about 6'5" and weighed at least 290 pounds. I'm screwed. What was I thinking? Knowing the only chance to beat him was to beat him to the punch, I sort of got a bit of a head start and slammed him down in about three seconds. A lot of the lookers-on laughed because the big old stud tackle was put down by little old me. The next thing I know, the big tackle reached over and grabbed my shirt and pulled me toward his face. He said in a low voice, more like a growl, "I'm going to find you and beat you to death." I wanted to tell him I thought he was a really good sport, but I kept my mouth shut … for once.

Throughout the year, when I wanted to go downtown to drink a beer, I always made sure to know where the exit was and always asked my buddies to yell at me if they see this monster come in and I'll run out the back door. I didn't want to die. The lookout system worked well until one night when I was having a good time in the Rocking R Bar. I felt this huge hairy hand on my shoulder pulling me toward none other than Mr. All Conference. "Finally, I get to kick your sorry little ass." My days on this earth are no doubt over.

He was pushing me out the back door, when suddenly we stopped. A big fullback on the football team said: "Leave the little dude alone. If you want to fight someone, fight me." Apparently, the big tackle wanted no part of the fullback. He only said: "OK, if you say so." Years later, I met the fullback at his bar in Kalispell and thanked him for saving my life. The monster tackle became a very successful head football coach and ended up being head coach at Purdue University. I met him a few years ago at the Purdue v. Notre Dame game in Lafayette, Indiana. During warm-ups, I talked the security guy into letting me say hello. "Hey Coach Joe, I'm a Bobcat. I just wanted to say hello and let you know I'm the guy that beat you in the arm-wrestling contest." "You are? You grew up! But you know you cheated." "I know – sorry. You sure have had a great coaching career. You're some coach." "I appreciate that. Good luck to you. I've got a game to coach." They beat Notre Dame.

My Sigma Chi brothers were a great bunch that studied hard but managed to play even harder. As an example, four of us Sigs decided to head out to West Yellowstone Park for a spring weekend of partying. The driver, Gary, had an old station wagon that could haul all of our sorry butts and a lot of booze. Instead of drinking our usual Buckhorn beer, one dollar and forty-nine cents a six-pack, we decided to get fancy and drink Country Club malt liquor. Going to West, we drank the malt liquor like it was beer. We started feeling really good, really fast because Country Club had 8% alcohol content, rather than our beer at 3%.

We managed to get into the park and as we passed by a bunch of bison, Henry asked Gary to stop. Henry had convinced himself, being somewhat of a cowboy, that he could ride a bison. A bison is about twelve hundred pounds of mean. The old buff lowered his head and had a look in his eye that you just knew he was ready to charge. Henry came to what was left of his senses and ran for the fence, getting under it in record time. I've never heard of anyone riding a bison, and I know a lot of cowboys. They are all smarter than to try.

We went further into the park, and Ric, the most conservative member of our group, said he wanted to get a closer look at one of the steaming hot geysers. We didn't know he brought a box of Tide in his duffel bag. Jumping out of the car with his box of Tide in hand, he ran to the geyser and dumped the box of tide into it. I'll never know what possessed him to do that. I guess he thought Yellowstone Park was one huge laundromat. He took his sweatshirt off, dipped it in the boiling water and pretended to wash it. Sober, we would have thought it was stupid, but we were more than halfway in the bag and thought it was hilarious. What little sense we had left told us to get Bucky back to the car before all of us were arrested and probably on national news. Some of the tourists thought Bucky's escapade was very funny. I guess you had to be there.

We were getting hungry, so we stopped at a restaurant just at the outskirts of West Yellowstone. We stuffed our faces with a lunch of burgers and fries and piled back into the station wagon. Henry, who almost rode a bison, said: "Look what I have." Crap! He took a Park Ranger hat and put it on his melon. We laughed at the goofball as he looked silly as hell. Even in the fog I was in, I knew that hat could get us all arrested. It wasn't easy, but we finally talked Henry into taking the hat back. Henry got out of the car, went up to the window where the Ranger was having lunch. He tapped on the window, put the Ranger's hat on and did a little dance. It looked sort of like a jig. After twirling around a couple of times, he put the hat on the ground and ran back to the car. We got out of there as fast as we could. The rest of the afternoon and evening, we kept looking over our shoulders to see if a bunch of rangers were coming to arrest us.

Later that night, I got into a poker game in the back of what was known as a dive. There was a bunch of locals in the game. They looked like they came out of the movie Deliverance. Quickly, I knew I was in a crooked game. There was a whole lot of blinking, tapping and scratching going on to tip off cards. This game wasn't my first rodeo. Even though I knew it was rigged, I stayed in for five hands. I lost all my money.

The guy next to me had to have been a big old logger whose hands were as big as dinner plates. I asked him to loan me $20.00 and that my friends would pay him back double if I lost the $20. Old toothless handed me the $20 bill with a shit-eating grin on his homely puss. I thanked him, got up and bolted out the front door, cash in hand. The rest of the night, I kept a lookout for one irritated logger. He never caught up with me or I wouldn't be writing this book.

I remember riding out of West Yellowstone and parking in some trees. We all had sleeping bags. I stuffed myself into mine and fell asleep. I woke up with somebody kicking me. I pried my eyes open and looked up. I was looking directly at a big old star on the side of a highway patrolman's car. The highway patrolman standing over me said: "Jesus, I thought you were dead. What the hell are you doing sleeping in the middle of the highway?" I did my best to explain: "There was a party I had with three of my fraternity brothers. Where are they?" His response: "I don't know, but I think I could track them down. I don't know what to do with you! I guess I could give you a ticket for littering the highway. Maybe for blocking the highway traffic. I'm going to let you off the hook, but promise me you'll behave yourself." "I'm going back to Bozeman and I could give you a ride." "Nah, I'll be ok." "Get into the barrow pit if you're going to sleep some more." He drove off. He was just happy I was alive.

I crawled over to a barrow pit and went back to sleep. I woke to the sound of my name, Sports Grape, a nickname I wanted them to forget. It sounded like they were pretty far away. Looking in the direction of the calls, I noticed a trail of down feathers leading into the trees. I had somehow ripped my sleeping bag and it left a trail I could easily follow back to the station wagon. I told them what happened. Henry piped up: "Holy shit, Grape, semi's drive into West on that road." "All I can figure was I must have been sleeping dead center in the highway. Also, no doubt I was passed out rather than snoozing."

We decided we had better mosey back to Bozeman and show some restraint. We figured we were lucky to not be in jail or, in my case, dead. I promised myself I would never drink Country Club again, or borrow money from toothless loggers, or sleep on any more highways, or go near any geysers with any type of laundry soap. I kept three out of four of those promises.

I did a bit of golfing while attending MSU. Golfing at the Riverside golf course, I hit a ball into a small stream that went into a pond. At the end of the pond, I could see a ton of golf balls collecting on the bottom, held in place by a metal screen. I had a frat brother who was a stud duck. He was very strong and even tougher, and he was a scuba diver. The little light bulb in my brain turned on – It would be a piece of cake to dive into the pond and collect hundreds of golf balls.

We decided to wait until midnight on a Wednesday to drive to the golf course, jump over the fence and head for the golf balls. We both had fins and snorkels. In no time, we had a big gunny sack filled with golf balls. We thought we were pretty damn smart as we hauled the balls over to our car. All of a sudden, lights came on, as well as a police siren. Out stepped two policemen shining their flashlights in our eyes. We were caught red-handed. They never told us who turned us in. I thought, this is it, I'm going to be arrested, thrown out of school, and maybe tarred and feathered.

We lucked out. We had to give the golf balls back, apologize to the manager of the golf course and turn ourselves into the dean of men at the university. The dean, at the very least, was no doubt going to tell us to go home. It was hard to believe, but all we had to do was be on probation for a quarter and stay out of trouble from then on. I always thought that because the dean was a Sigma Chi alum, that sort of helped our cause. Truthfully, I know it did.

My final year at MSU and my fifth year in college was semi-tame with a few notable exceptions. Through handball, I made friends with the head wrestling coach, Herb Acox. I asked him if I could try out for the Bobcat wrestling team. "How much experience have you had wrestling?" "None." "You know you're going to get beat up and killed, right?" "Probably, but I want to coach wrestling someday and what better way to learn?" "You're still going to get killed!" I promised Herb that I would do everything they were doing, never complain, and that I wouldn't quit, no matter what. Talk about a steep learning curve! This was beyond steep. It was helpful that several of my Sigma Chi brothers were on the wrestling team, and they gave me some extra coaching. After the first week, everything on my body hurt, even my hair. I hung in there, but sometimes wondered if all of the concussions I accumulated made me do senseless stuff. Herb said if I kept improving, he could possibly get me a partial scholarship. "Hey Herb, I'm a fifth year senior! I need to get a job." "I didn't think you were at MSU that long." He didn't know about the two years I spent at Carroll.

In November, my golf ball diver Don, and a big old goof by the name of Charley Klimax (it's really Klimas) decided to go duck hunting on the famous Madison River. We went to the Army Navy Store and rented a raft for twenty bucks. Cromer had a '54 Volkswagen that was our transportation. Getting the raft roped onto the top of the little car took some doing. It was zero degrees when we took off. No doubt there would be some ice on the river. We parked, hauled the raft down to the river and started paddling. We floated about a half a mile with Charley in front paddling and trying to keep the raft somewhere near the middle of the river. Don and I were ready to shoot anything with the right type of feathers on. Going around a bend, a flock of geese flew over us. I got off two quick shots and whiffed both. All of a sudden, I heard a loud ripping sound and saw the front of the raft coming over the top of us. Down we went into the freezing water of the Madison. I swam as hard as I could for shore. Getting there, I saw Charley clinging onto a big cottonwood branch. He was hanging on for dear life. We didn't know he didn't know how to swim. Cromer easily swam to shore. The raft was sunk and long gone. Then it hit me – my father's favorite shotgun was now residing at the bottom of the Madison. This could mean my demise. I told Don what happened. "No sweat, I'll dive down and get it!" "Go downstream and about thirty yards and try to stop me as I come through." The river was running swiftly where we were. Don dove into the icy water, surfaced just in front of me – I caught him. "I almost had it. I'm going to try again." On the second attempt, he came up with shotgun in hand. A miracle! Now, we had another problem. Charley had a death grip on the cottonwood. Don and I waded into the water and grabbed his legs to pull him towards the shoreline. We got him to pry loose from the tree. By now, we looked like human ice cubes.

We took off running back to the Volkswagen. On the way back, a big cow moose was directly in our path to the car. Yelling our fool heads off, we didn't break stride and ran directly toward Mrs. Moose. Thank the good lord, she stepped out of our way. We decided getting mauled by a moose wasn't as bad as freezing to death. The three large ice cubes managed to reach the Volkswagen and turn the heater on full blast. Old Volkswagen heaters suck! It took what seemed like forever to thaw us out. Add rafting on the Madison in November to my list of things never to do again. Not so cool that we had to buy a sunken raft at the bottom of the Madison. At least I got dad's shotgun back.

During my final year at MSU, I actually studied a lot. I raised my grade point to over 3.3. A week before I was set to graduate, I received a notice from MSU's administration office that I couldn't graduate because I didn't fulfill a 2-year ROTC requirement. My heart stopped for a while. Once it started again, I literally ran the two miles to the Admin Building in record time. I found my friend, the Dean of Men, and explained to him that I am still in the Marine Corps, so I am not required to do ROTC. He said he would straighten this out. I was able to graduate on time. To this day, I still have nightmares about not being able to graduate.

CHAPTER 9

A Few Good Men

I'm not sure what I was thinking when I decided to enlist in the Marine Corps. The Corps had a program, mainly for college guys, that allowed you to go through boot camp, then advanced boot camp called "Second ITR" during the summers. After going through those programs, you then went to Quantico, Virginia, for an officers training program. Their hope, if you met their standards, was that you would sign up for five years, starting at the rank of Second Lieutenant. You could opt out, but you had a six-year reserve commitment to fulfill.

My cousin, Burt Zumberg, was a highly decorated marine who was wounded saving his best friend's life during the Korean War. He was awarded the Silver Star. With my admiration for him, and thinking I was sort of a tough guy, it seemed like a good idea to sign up. I drove to Butte, America, and signed up. Shortly thereafter, I found myself on a plane flying to Los Angeles and then being bussed to a lonely little spot in the desert called Camp Pendleton to start boot camp. There was a lovely little greeting party anxiously awaiting our arrival. I could tell by looking around at some of the guys that were on the bus that they were scared shitless. Call me stupid or crazy, but I wasn't one of them, as I had a good idea of what to expect. I couldn't imagine my Drill Instructor being tougher on me than my dad was.

Getting off the bus, they, the D.I.'s, made us stand on a platform so they could begin breaking us down through humiliation and intimidation. They said in no uncertain terms that the two of us from Montana were "sheep fuckers." Neither one of us was too bothered by this, but when they called us "chicken fuckers," that stung just a bit.

I soon learned that D.I.'s could use the word "fuck" in a variety of ways. It could easily be a verb as in "fuck you bunch of maggots." They seemed to have a thing for maggots and shit birds. "You are a bunch of fuckers," I guess is a noun. And, well you get the picture. One last example, "you bunch of fuckers could fuck up a fucking two-car parade even if you had a fucking map showing you where the fucking parade was heading the fuck to." I'm nowhere as proficient as they were at using the "F" word. Growing up, that's a word that was hardly ever heard or used. Also, if you gave someone the finger, that meant you wanted to get into a fist fight. Now, even little old ladies flip people off. So sad!

Back to my first day as a would-be marine. When we got to our Quonset hut, where we were going to lunch, I suddenly got the idea of what minorities felt like, because about eighty-five percent of our platoon and Company were black. In Deer Lodge, we had only one black family and their name was Brown. They were nice quiet people who bothered no one. I just started to unpack my gear and one of the blacks called me "Whitey." I told him, "Sorry, but my name is Ken." His response was: "Fuck you, white boy." He didn't know he was messing with a prison city kiddie. I cordially invited him to join me behind the head, marine talk for restroom, after dark. The biggest one of the bunch seemed more than happy to accept my challenge. By nineteen, I had learned to brawl pretty well, so I outlasted him and took a pretty good beating in doing so. I wasn't called Whitey again.

I always liked doing sit-ups, pushups, and pullups. When I messed up, which was quite often, the D.I.'s typically made me do seventy-five pushups. I could do seventy-five fairly easily. This seemed to really irritate one of the D.I.s, who wanted to teach me a lesson by standing on me while I tried to do the pushups. I gave it everything I had, to no avail. Maybe if he was fifty pounds, I could have finished seventy-five. Actually, I was really good at the physical fitness tests and ended up second in our Company. On the downside, I ended up in the lowest quartile in leadership qualities. The Corps definitely didn't want me thinking for myself – sort of: "this way or no way."

At one point, I was a Lance Corporal and when I was honorably discharged, I was a private first class, second to lowest on the totem pole. Here's how that happened.

During about the middle of boot camp, we had to bivouac in the hills above Pendleton after we marched about five miles in really hot weather. That evening, I noticed some very stupid D.I.s were making their platoon pitch their tents in poison ivy. What in the hell were they thinking? I knew that they were smarter than that. It had to be intentional. The next morning, none of those poor souls could even open their eyes, they were so swollen up, let alone breathe without gasping for air. I didn't mind, and understood all the strenuous straining, the yelling and berating, but what they did made no sense to me and really made me upset.

We stayed out for two nights doing night exercises. Piece of cake, I could see really well at night. The next morning before heading back, our fearless Captain chewed us out, on general principle, for being a bunch of pussies. All due respect to pussies, but I knew he only had empty milk cartons in his pack. Also, he was wearing running shoes. Of course, we had forty-five-pound packs, one rifle and heavy boots on for the march back to the base. It was about a three-mile, double-time march back to the asphalt grinder, which was our final destination. My attitude was horrible. I had impetigo on my face, so when I shaved, I would almost bleed to death. I had a fairly heavy beard, so sometimes I had to shave twice a day to pass inspections. This condition did nothing to improve my attitude.

My buddy from Hamilton, Montana, and I decided that we will show the old bugger who is in shape and who is not. We stayed where we belonged behind Captain Running Shoes and then, when we were about three quarters of a mile from the grinder, we fell out of rank and ran like hell for the grinder. Breaking rank is bad enough, but being the really smart guys that we were, we had to make some wise-ass remarks as we passed by him. We reached the grinder way ahead of our Company. We laughed our fool heads off until the reality of what we just did set in hard and both of us knew "holy shit, this is going to hurt."

We were immediately escorted into the officer's Quonset hut where three Second Lieutenants proceeded to play let's-see-who-can-slam-these-two-maggots-against-the-walls the hardest. I seemed to bounce off the walls better than my buddy. It's a contest I didn't want to be in.

They either got bored with slamming us around or they took pity on us for being morons. For the next phase of our punishment, for the next ten days, we had to carry buckets of water uphill to the latrine, which was about a hundred yards away. They made it a lot harder by telling us we had to carry the buckets with our arms extended straight out from our sides. We were told to water the ice plants surrounding the latrine. By the way, I wanted to tell them that ice plants don't require watering but, for once, I kept my trap shut.

Our first trip up the hill, our arms damn near fell off. We were sweating like little pigs and thought this would be a horrible way to die. I didn't want my buddies hearing that I died in the Marine Corps from carrying water buckets to a latrine. Before the second trip up, we didn't think anyone was paying attention to us, so we decided to only fill the buckets halfway. It worked! The third trip, our buckets were empty except for some water splashed on the outside of the buckets. Luckily, we never got caught. I couldn't imagine what would have happened to us if we were. The Corps wasn't fond of cheating.

One of the training exercises we did was to learn to use pugil sticks. They are just a wooden rod with canvas pads stuck on the ends. It was, I guess, supposed to simulate close combat using a rifle. For some unknown reason, I was really good at using these things. Sometimes, I would grab the stick by the end or swing it like a baseball bat. Oftentimes, if the opponent charged me, I would drop down hoping they would fall over me, then I would jump up and pummel the unsuspecting boot camper into submission. I totally ignored what I was taught by the D.I.s, but guess what? I kept winning and eventually became the Company middle weight champion. Because of my success, we, our platoon, were granted twenty-four hours leave. We couldn't leave the base, but we got to go to the PX and stuff ourselves with candy bars. On Monday morning, we paid the price for our gluttony on our four-thirty run before breakfast. Candy bars were called Pogey bait. To this day, I have no idea why they were called this.

At the end of bootcamp, we all were called Marines instead of maggots, shitheads, sheep molesters, etc. We were all relieved to rise above maggot status. So, I'm standing outside on the grinder waiting to see where I would be assigned. I was an 0300, which I discovered was a ground pounder, or if you want to be fancy, an infantryman.

We, our platoon, all got their assignments except guess who – yours truly. The D.I., with a smirk on his face, told me to stay put until they could get this straightened out. He said I had to do everything the new boot campers had to do, only they wouldn't yell at me anymore. I guess they were tired of yelling at me. I thought it would be a day or two until I got my assignment, but no, it was almost four weeks before I was assigned to what was called Second I.T.R. at Camp San Onofre. It was an advanced boot camp, but without all the swearing at us and we learned some pretty cool ways to kill the enemy.

Because I was stronger than most of my fellow Marines, I was selected to carry the Browning Automatic rifle, the B.A.R. for short. It weighed about twenty-three pounds and was fun to fire, especially at night with tracers, so you could see where the bullets were landing. I actually had a fairly good time in Second I.T.R.

After completion of advanced bootcamp, I was sent to Quantico, Virginia, to find out if I was officer material. We were located next to the F.B.I. center and some recon maniacs. The reconnaissance nuts ran everywhere, and I am not sure if they ever slept.

During the second night at Quantico, our platoon was visited at one in the morning by a shellshocked Korean War Sergeant. He would turn on the lights and walk through our hut tapping on our racks with a swagger stick while we stood at attention. Other times, he would push our double bunks over onto the cement floor. He was such a joy.

About the third week, old shellshocked arrived around midnight and made us stand at attention. He would walk between the lines and inspect us for God knows what reason. Down the line he came, looking us up and down. The hombre across from me had a sizable hard-on. I watched intently as the old Sergeant arrived at Mr. Boner's spot. He looked at Boner's eyes and then looked down to see old one-eyed trouser mouse in all of its majesty. Old Sarge jumped back like he had just encountered a poisonous snake. That did it for me. I burst out laughing and I couldn't stop. The old bugger told our D.I. about my disrespectful behavior. I suggested to our fearless D.I. that he probably would have laughed too. It did no good.

My punishment for my sense of humor was to stand outside at attention with my helmet on backwards. Lucky me, it rained all night for both the nights I was standing, or sometimes slouching, at semi-attention. Quantico is hot and muggy in the daytime, but really cold at night and I'm from Montana where it's frequently forty below. I guess it's the humidity.

Quantico is home of the Marine Corps track team. Every morning at 4 A.M., a long-legged Second Lieutenant, who had to be on the track team, showed up to lead us on laps. We all had to move more than double time to keep up with him. Being no dummy, I knew it was really dark at 4 A.M. So, after one lap, I saw a knoll surrounding the track we were doing the laps on, and I decided to go over the knoll and stay there until the final lap and then join in the fun. A couple of my buddies on the second morning joined me. The word got out, and a whole bunch of slackers were joining us. On the fourth morning, the Second Lieutenant looked back and only about a fourth of the platoon was behind him. Thinking for yourself is not in the Marine Corps training bible and I know why that is. You have to follow orders or too many people die. It was still fun while it lasted.

At Quantico, our platoon consistently had high marks when inspections came. We had an advantage. Instead of washing our stuff with these little scrub boards, we made a great discovery. Lo and behold, we saw that there were automatic washing machines by the enlisted men's Quonset hut. We were lucky that we never got caught using them.

I didn't get into any major trouble for the rest of the time I spent at Quantico. During the last week of training, I had a big decision to make. I had to decide if I wanted to become an officer and sign up for five years or not. By this time, I was convinced that we had made a big mistake by being in Vietnam. After a lot of agonizing, trying to decide what to do, I decided to opt out.

For all of boot camp, second I.T.R. and officer training camp, I was constantly told what a mess I was and totally unfit to be an officer. Shoot, I was told I was unfit to be a private, let alone a Second Lieutenant. So, I thought opting out shouldn't be any problem. I'll just waltz into the Company Commander's office and let the Captain know my decision. Well, it wasn't that easy. The Captain said I had to have a good reason. Being the quick thinker I was, I blurted out that I wanted to become a priest. He said, and I quote, "Bullshit." Desperate for a better reason, I tried, "I think I'm queer." His response: "double bullshit." I stood my ground and said: "For months, I've been told I wasn't worth spit, so now all of a sudden I'm the next Chesty Puller?" (Chesty was a highly honored and respected Marine officer).

The Captain told me to get the hell out of his office and go see Major so-and-so. I reported to Major so-and-so. He told me I couldn't opt out unless I had a really good reason. Being desperate, I tried a new strategy. "Major sir, I think I'm probably the biggest chicken shit in the world." All he said was, "your record indicates otherwise." He sent me to see a Lieutenant Colonel. Geez, I was starting to think I would have to be a four-star general before I'm done. Nothing worked so far, so what the hell, maybe honesty is the best policy for exercising my rights. When the Colonel asked why, I simply said: "I know my rights according to the contract I signed, and I do not want to be an officer. I think I have a time commitment of more Second I.T.R. and then a six-year reserve commitment. As best I can, I will do my duty as an enlisted soldier." All he said was: "Sign here and be on your way. Dismissed." As a little punishment, they kept me isolated for ten days before sending me home.

I was almost certain that sometime during the next six years, I would be called in to serve active duty in Vietnam. In the fifth year of fulfilling my reserve commitment, I was teaching and coaching in my hometown and was married with three daughters, when I was mailed an official looking letter from the United States Marine Corps. I thought: "This is it; I'm going to Nam." My heart pounding, I quickly opened the letter. Basically, it stated that my Reserve Unit in Billings, Montana, had been deactivated, therefore your reserve commitment has been fulfilled. Also enclosed is your honorable discharge. Why wasn't I called to duty? The reason the reserve unit was deactivated was because the Corps had called so many from the Unit to go to Vietnam that they had to close it down. Again, why not me? To this day, I still wonder why I wasn't called to go.

I went downtown to a local watering hole to celebrate my good fortune. My next-door neighbor went with me. I remember drinking shots of tequila about as fast as humanly possible. I woke up at three in the morning to discover I had been sleeping in my neighbor's bathtub. Two good things: he was next-door and he was driving. It was a long day at the good old high school trying to inspire a bunch of juniors and seniors to love history and government. Because of losing several fraternity brothers and friends to the war in Vietnam, I wish I had been called up to serve there. Because I didn't, I never asked for any benefits for which vets are qualified.

CHAPTER 10

I Wanted to Be A Coach

I was assigned to do my student teaching in White Sulphur Springs, Montana, a small ranching and logging community at the base of the Castle Mountains in south central Montana. I knew that there was terrific hunting and fishing in this area. I also knew that the winters were cold enough to freeze the balls off a brass monkey. Now that's cold! Lucky for me, I got to stay in the home of one of my Sigma Chi brothers, Ric Buckingham. Ric's dad was a successful rancher. His mom was the nicest lady and the best cook in America. Ric's Aunt Gert lived with the Buckinghams. Aunt Gert was an intelligent lady who made a lot of money investing in the stock market. Gert was also head of the entertainment department. The first evening, she asked me what mixed drink I liked. Being mostly a beer drinker, I could only think of Tom Collins. Two nights later, after dinner, we began our ritual of downing a few highballs and visiting about sports, news, and the stock market. I found out that she purchased a case of gin and a case of Tom Collins mix to make sure we didn't run short.

Every evening, Ric's father would arrive home with mud on his shit-kickers and would be greeted with: "Don't go any further with those muddy boots on." "The muddy boots are the reason you have this nice house and lots of money!" Never in my life was I ever treated as well as I was by the Buckinghams.

Because I loved to hunt and fish and had a chance to do some coaching, when offered a teaching position at White Sulphur, I took it. My supervising teacher when I was student teaching was a short, stocky, bulldog-type of guy, Gary Rafter. He reminded me of a pit bull. I liked and respected him. He knew I wanted to coach football and he was tired of it, so he said: "Let's be co-head coaches. When we win, I'll be the head coach and when we lose, you'll be head coach. Deal?"

During the first practice session, I started lining up the players by position. Boy did I get a lot of strange looks: "What's going on?" "Coach, you're putting eleven men on the field, and we play eight-man football." Oh boy, I had a lot to learn in a hurry!

My teaching assignment was to try to instruct 28 seventh and eighth graders. On the first day, I noticed a really large eighth-grader. All of six foot and one hundred eighty pounds. Also, he was sixteen years old. I wanted to get to know each student a little bit better, so I asked them what they wanted to do for a living when they grew up. The six-footer said: "I want to be a jockey." Being the smart ass that I was, I asked him what was he going to ride, an elephant? I could tell by the absence of any light in his eyes that he didn't have a clue what I was trying to get across.

It didn't take long to discover that this was the meanest, nastiest bunch of little snots known to mankind. Our Superintendent was 6'6" and 270 pounds, the Assistant Principal ended up Dean of Men at Oregon State, the assistant football coach, who helped try to control this bunch, was 6'2" and 230 pounds and tough as hell, and all of us had our hands full keeping control of this group. Of course, not all of the bunch were miscreants, but the majority were.

During one noon hour, looking out the window, I saw one of the boys out in the field behind the Junior High building and clearly he was trying to rape a seventh grade girl. I ran as fast as I could, and when I reached him, I barreled into him with everything I had. That ended all his desire for sex. This little man grew up and left White Sulphur and went to California. I was told that he ran over and killed a highway patrolman and was sentenced to life in prison.

Later in my education career, I handled most of the discipline in a high school with 2100 students, easier than this sorry bunch. Again, there were a few really good kids in the two grades. I felt sorry for them. They deserved better.

The second year in W.S.S., I was head football coach by myself. After being in W.S.S. for a year, I came to realize that more booze was consumed per capita here than any place in the world. After athletic contests, it was expected, win or lose, for the coaches to go to the bars to have more than a few drinks with the locals. The favorite watering hold was the Melody Lane, and it was owned and operated by the Chairman of the school board.

Knowing how much drinking was going on, I should have known better than to try to enforce training rules. Our first game, we went to Stanford, Montana, on Friday afternoon and we won easily. Our big 6'2" and 190 pound running back, who loved contract, ran roughshod over our opponents. He was what we call a helmet-breaker. Get this, his name was Dudley Deal. No kidding!

One Sunday evening, some of my friends let me know that the football players had been partying all weekend. Before Monday's practice, I told all of the players to go sit in the bleachers. It seemed like they knew what was coming. Not a lot of eye contact. "You know the training rules. Anyone who was out drinking this weekend, step out of the bleachers and turn your equipment in." Nobody moved. After what seemed like a lifetime, finally a little sophomore got up and slowly walked into the locker room to turn in his gear. A few minutes later, three seniors left. Then almost half the team got up and left, including Mr. Deal. Dudley stopped on the way out and said: "What's the big deal? We only were drinking on Friday and Saturday night. We didn't even go out on Sunday night." The youngest brother of the Chairman of the Board was one of the partiers. Now, I had to patch together a team made up of mostly freshman and sophomores. The rest of the season was a nightmare. Our next opponent was the Belgrade Panthers. They had a great team led by a 6', 210-pound fullback. Their head coach was a friend of mine. I explained our situation. "Please tell your fullback not to run over our 115-pound freshman safety." "Coach, you have my word. I'll tell him to run around, not over, him." He kept his word. We managed to finish the season without any of my little guys getting any major injuries. There were a lot of really good athletes in town. Unfortunately, they were twenty to thirty years old!

During my three years at White Sulphur Springs, there were a couple of positive things I was involved in. I was elected President of the Jaycees. Rather than spend money on badges or conventions, I found out how much money we had, and spent every last nickel on buying glasses and food for every family that couldn't afford to buy glasses or didn't have enough to eat. Because I zeroed out our funds, we had to do a fundraiser. White Sulphur gets a ton of snow. "Let's do a snowmobile rally." We had the ideal location to hold the races, just ten miles north of town. We had a great response with over a hundred snowmobiles signing up for the event. Everything was going along splendidly, until I got a bright idea. Thinking a lot of snowmobilers were doughboys that were fat, I came up with a way to reward the more fit contestants. A La Mans start! We would line up all of the racers, fifty yards from their snowmobiles. At the gun, they were to race to their machines, hop on and start the race. There was about three feet of snow on the level. I raised the starting gun and Bam, off they went. Well, sort of. A few of the really chubby ones went about ten feet and fell into the snow gasping for air. One of my Jaycee friends yelled: "Shit, Ken, you're going to kill all of them." I started to pray: "Please lord, don't let any of the chubbies die." Thank God, a doctor was a Jaycee and was helping at the race. Out of about seventy racers, only twenty-four got to their machines. The other fifty-some were too pooped to run me down. I made myself scarce for the rest of the rally. I could just see the headlines in the local newspaper: "Race director pummeled to death by a bunch of fat snowmobilers!"

During the years I was in W.S.S., I drank way, way too much, was just barely OK as a teacher, was a pretty good track coach and was a mediocre football coach. I was happy to leave White Sulphur Springs.

A friend of mine who was head football coach in Roundup, Montana, told me I ought to apply for his job as he was leaving to go to Missoula. He said: "We're loaded with great players. All you have to do is sit back and watch them win." I applied and came in second out of thirty-eight applicants. The Roundup team went on to win 34 straight games. They picked the right guy to lead them.

Still looking for my next teaching job, I found out that my hometown had an opening for a social studies teacher and assistant football and wrestling coach in the high school. I applied, and got the job. One of the worst mistakes of my life! You'll see why by the time you finish this chapter.

I thought it would be great to go back to Deer Lodge as a teacher and coach. I vowed to be a better person and a much better educator than I was at White Sulphur. Truthfully, I was shocked that I was hired, based on my behavior while a high school student at P.C.H.S. Folks had to have had very short memories or they were very forgiving.

Powell County High School had just hired a new superintendent who, we found out, was spending a lot of time working on his doctorate degree. The school district provided a house for him that was located next to the high school. I mention this because he spent more time there during the day than he did at the school.

It's always exciting to meet your students on the first day of school, especially in your hometown when you know just about everyone in your classes. My first period class was held in the auditorium. That seemed odd. I was scheduled to teach American History to juniors. Walking into the room, I saw ninety smiley-faced juniors staring at me.

Ninety!! I asked them if they were having a class meeting. The son of the family that grew up next door to us said: "Nope, Ken, I mean Mr. Colbo. We're all in your American History Class!" It didn't help that new textbooks were ordered and hadn't arrived. Somehow, this is a mistake that will soon be corrected, hopefully.

Second period I had to supervise a study hall with about 100 mostly bored students in it. I could deal with that. Third period was my prep period. Oh, oh! My fourth period Government Class for seniors was to be held in the auditorium. Walking in, I was greeted by one hundred seniors who were raising hell before I stepped in. Stepping up on to the stage, I saw a sea of inquisitive faces. "You in the front row, is this a senior class meeting or is this Senior Government class?" "It's your government class" came the answer. He was grinning like a Cheshire Cat. Again, there weren't any textbooks to be seen. Asking if they had textbooks, several in the audience said no! Let me get this straight – I have almost the entire senior class, no textbooks, in an auditorium right before lunch. This is about as bad as it can get.

During the noon hour, I finally found the Superintendent and asked him: "What the hell is going on with my teaching assignment?" "Relax, textbooks have been ordered and will be here in a few weeks! Also, I will get you some assistants to help you with your Junior American History and the Senior Government class."

I found out the good old Rodger the Dodger used a computer to schedule classes. He obviously didn't know what he was doing. He was so busy writing his thesis for his doctorate, he actually forgot to order any textbooks. No big deal ... for him. I never got any help from assistants, but at least textbooks finally came in. Three months late, of course. This joke of a superintendent would be fired after one year. I assume he received his doctorate and would bless some poor unsuspecting school district with his presence.

Coaching wasn't much better than teaching. The first year, I was an assistant football and wrestling coach. That was actually O.K. My second year, I became head football and wrestling coach. Football became a nightmare. One of my assistant coaches was the old track coach who wanted me to be his manager. Years ago, he was fired from being the head football and basketball coach. He spent the rest of his career trying to undermine the football and basketball programs. How sad!

I was trying to run a modern-day offense in football, and I expected all of my assistants to do the same. The old track coach, when I checked on his practices with the J.V. squad, was running what was called the spinner series, which was used in the late forties. In those days, linebackers didn't cross the line of scrimmage. The spinner offense had the quarterback turn his back to the line of scrimmage, while the backs crossed behind him. In other words, this antiquated offense would guarantee the quarterback would end up in the hospital or worse. I told him to start running my offense. Part of his assignment was to do some scouting for me. I asked him to go to Polson, Montana, and scout the Pirates who I was pretty sure had a solid team. On Monday, at our coaches' meeting, I asked Chuck for his scouting report and he said: "They are terrible, so I didn't take any notes. You won't have any problem with them." Polson beat us fifty-six to twelve and went on to play in the state championship, losing by a point to Butte Central 7-6. I don't think he even went to Polson. I sure appreciated Uncle Chuckie's help. You just can't have a winning program unless the entire staff is on the same page.

My second year coaching the football team, I played a bunch of sophomores. The juniors and seniors were not very big, and made up for that by being really slow. We got the snot knocked out of us at first, but I could see the younger players getting better and better. Our last game, we went to Dillon, Montana. We beat them fifty-six to six. Within a week, Dillon fired their coach. I used to stop in Dillon on my way to go fishing in Clark Canyon Reservoir. There was a restaurant where all the local sports fans hung out. Stepping in for breakfast, I saw a group of parents hashing over the local gossip. I knew a couple of the parents. They told me how glad they were to get rid of their terrible coach. I said: "You're not going to like what I'm going to say, but your coach didn't have any really good players. In fact, not only were they not very good, but were actually very poor. You made a mistake firing him." "You don't know what you're talking about." "Well, we will see." Swede Kennison, the terrible coach, went on to be head coach at Butte Central. He won thirty-eight straight games and won three state championships. Stopping in at the same restaurant a few years later, I recognized a couple of the parents who were so happy to fire Swede. I told them: "Swede sure got a lot smarter about coaching when he moved eighty miles east to Butte!" They were speechless.

When I left Deer Lodge, I told the incoming football coach that he must bring in his own assistants or he could never win. He told me he knew about the really good junior class, and he thought he could win no matter who they assigned to him. He lost every game and was fired in November. Leaving Deer Lodge, he had a very long and successful coaching career in Western Montana.

Not only were my teaching assignments a disaster, but I noticed that I was only getting about two miles per gallon on my pickup. Somebody was siphoning gas out of the pickup. I always parked in front of my house. My plan was to turn out the lights in my living room, leave the front door open a little and look out the front window to try to catch the thief. Nothing happened for the first two nights. On the third night, I saw a dark figure sneaking up to my truck. I quietly creeped up to my front door. I remember thinking that this could be fun! I waited until I saw the hose go into the gas tank and then I snuck up on the culprit, waiting for him to suck on the hose. When he did, I wrapped my arms around him and squeezed as hard as I could. Yahoo! He swallowed some gas and was trembling with fright. I threw him on the ground and told him not to move. Out of the corner of my eye, I saw another person running down the street. Looking close-up at the shaking body on the ground, I realized I was looking at my next-door neighbor's son, who was a senior in high school. I took him next door and woke his father up to let him know what was going on.

It turned out that there were three seniors involved, two lookouts and the guzzler. On their last day of school, the little snots left me a note. It said that they wanted to meet me after school in an open lot behind the school. They also said that they were going to beat the crap out of me. I made sure they were all eighteen or older. They were. I thought about it a lot, but I decided that I would show up just to see if they would. I waited about thirty to forty minutes and I guessed they changed their minds. I suspected it was a bunch of hot air. I was happy to leave Deer Lodge, just as I was happy to leave White Sulphur Springs.

Coaching and teaching in Deer Lodge was driving me nuts, so as a diversion, besides drinking, I went hunting for deer and especially elk. My father was an avid hunter who would get on an elk track and keep on it even if it meant staying overnight. I absolutely loved hunting. I, on the other hand, never liked killing animals, but I loved to chase them around. For a long time, our family lived on deer, elk, ducks, pheasants, grouse and a ton of fish.

Let me describe my main hunting buddies. The first one is Kurt. (I'll just use their first names as I don't know what I can get away with writing this book.) Kurt is a 6'3" cowboy who is as tough as a two-dollar steak. The next one, Gary, is a fraternity brother who thinks everyone is a soup sandwich. He is 6'3" and about 230 pounds. He has a nice little beer gut going. I affectionally called him Kettle Belly. The last one is Gary, who I coached when he was playing Babe Ruth baseball. At age thirteen, he was 6'2" and had a hell of an arm. Standing only 45 feet away from the hitter on the pitcher's mound, he scared the crap out of normal-sized Babe-Ruthers. Most of the little buggers were damn glad to get out of the batter's box alive. He ended up being 6'6" and well over 300 pounds. He blew out his shoulder playing college football. If that hadn't happened, I have no doubt he could have played in the NFL.

My three friends and I decided to go hunting in the Big Belt mountains in Central Montana. There are also the Little Belt mountains.

(Why are they called the Belts? I don't know.) We jumped in my four-wheel-drive Jeep station wagon and drove to Hobson, Montana, on Friday evening. We heard that there was the Utica bar just a few miles from Hobson. The famous cowboy artist, Charlie Russell lived for a while in a cabin near Utica. We just had to have a few beers at the Utica Bar.

I was the first one to walk into the bar. My buddies were screwing around outside the bar. At the time, I wasn't really big but at 5'10" and 220 pounds, I wasn't exactly small. Looking around the bar, I saw four guys sitting at the bar and they sure didn't look like Montanans, the way they were outfitted. They had dude written all over them. Also, they were really drunk. The largest, rather fat guy, looked at me and said: "Hey little man, how 'bout buying a round of drinks for us, if you know what's good for you." "Sure, but wait just a minute for my three little friends to come in." Fatso said: "Good, then all of them can buy us drinks."

Kurt the raw-boned 6'3" cowboy came in. Kurt is the kind of guy that simply looks like ten miles of bad road. About a minute later, my 6'3" 240-pound friend who thought most folks were soup sandwiches entered the bar. Fatso and friends became quiet and appeared startled by the appearance of Kurt and Turf. The last to enter was Gary, all 6'6" and 320 pounds of him. He was wearing a ten-gallon cowboy hat that made him look like he was over seven feet tall. Gary always has a scowl on his face, even when he's happy. He just looks mad as hell most of the time.

By now, our four friends at the bar looked like they were being invaded by a bunch of grizzly bears. Before any of us could say a word,

Fatso stood up and said: "You look like a great bunch of guys, and we want to pay for whatever you want to drink for as long as you want to be here." Wow! I thought we just died and went to heaven.

I just knew what good old Turf had to say to our new friends: "You guys look like a bunch of soup sandwiches." Gary was much nicer, only saying: "Hello girls." I, however, being a gentleman said to the bartender: "We will have beers and shots back and just keep 'em coming." My rawhide cowboy asked them if they had ever seen a horse. They nodded that indeed they had. "Good, so you must know they don't look like elk." "Just making sure." I was so proud of how nice my hunting buddies could be if they really worked at it. We found out the fearsome foursome were from California. Gary, being an inquisitive type and anxious to start a confrontation, asked them if they were queers. We were not sophisticated enough to use the term gays. They quickly informed us that they were all happily married. Turf, wanting to be part of this discussion, asked them if they were married to each other. After a few rounds, we actually started to like them just a little bit. Hey, we even bought them a round before we called it a night and headed out the door. Before exiting, Gary, trying his best to leave a good impression, said: "Don't get lost or shoot any animals or yourselves in the butt." I thought, alright, that's very good advice and was also considerate. I would like to tell you that we all went hunting and each of us shot a six-point bull elk, but trying to be somewhat honest in writing this book, what I can say is that we had a really good time not being successful hunting that weekend.

I just remembered that we did have to drive across a fairly rapid stream to get to our camping spot. Gary, Turf and I crossed in my four-wheel drive station wagon. Zook was following us, driving his rear wheel little Mazda. We barely made it across. Zook looked over the situation and never in his life did he back down from a challenge, so he decided that if he backed up enough and floor boarded his little car, he could fly across the stream. All of us knew there was no way. We told him so. Undaunted, Zook backed way up and gunned the engine and much to our amazement, he almost made it. Water was up to his waist and his car floated downstream about fifty yards until he got high-centered on a sandbar. We were laughing so hard; we didn't even think about how he was going to get back across. Luckily, I had a come-along on my rig, so I could wench Zook's car out of the stream on to dry land. I knew damn well that he was going to try to vault across the stream again. He tried to convince us that he just needed a longer runway. Having enough time to be quite sober, we all started to worry that Kurt could seriously damage his car or himself. We also knew we couldn't talk him out of thinking he was Evel Knievel. He backed up as far as he could and again stomped on the gas pedal. He hit the bank at a high rate of speed and went airborne. The old 32 foot per second thing got him again as he landed smack dab in the middle of the stream again. Luckily, he was alive, and his water-logged car only drifted downstream about twenty yards and was stopped by a fair-sized log jam. This time, he was close enough to the bank that I could wrap a chain around his front bumper and drag him out of his newfound swimming hole. Climbing out of the drenched car, Kurt said: "If I had a longer runway, I could have made it!" I was surprised he didn't want a third try. After a couple of hours waiting for Kurt's waterlogged car to dry out, we went on our merry way. To this day, I smile every time I think about Kurt and his little car.

While coaching wrestling at Deer Lodge, I got the bright idea that I would enter a freestyle wrestling tournament held in Billings, Montana. I decided that I would wrestle in the 148-pound weight class. I weighed 210 pounds when I made this decision. Was I nuts? Why did I decide to lose over sixty pounds to be in the 148-pound class? I wanted to know what my wrestlers were going through when they were dieting. Also, I, being the sort of smart guy that I am, thought it would be easier to wrestle little guys. It didn't occur to me at the time that I would be a little guy too. I never said I was really smart, just *sort of* smart.

My diet consisted of a cup of coffee for breakfast, a hamburger patty and some vitamins for lunch and a salad for dinner. I worked out with my wrestlers and then ran the gym bleachers that were really steep, for up to two hours at a time with a plastic sweatshirt on. Now, if that's not really stupid, nothing is! After two months of this insanity, I was within two pounds of making weight. The next morning, I woke up and all of my glands were swollen. I immediately went to see my doctor. Because I was so paranoid about losing weight, I hardly drank any water causing my kidneys to shut down. My doctor said I was going to die if I didn't rest and drink a lot of fluids. He gave me some kind of medicine to take.

Following his orders, I drank as much water as I could and stayed in bed for twenty-four hours. Nothing happened. Even though I felt like crap, I got out of bed and walked around a little bit. About three hours after I got up, I had to pee, thank goodness. I started peeing and peeing and peeing some more. I must have set some sort of record.

When I finally got rid of all the retained fluid, I weighed 149 pounds. I decided, to hell with it, I'm going to lose another pound and head to Billings and try my luck at freestyle wrestling.

I checked into a motel the night before the meet and bought a Billings Gazette, the local paper to see if they had an article about the freestyle event. I turned to the sports section and staring me right in my face was the headline: "Deer Lodge mat coach gets a chance to practice what he preaches." The first paragraph told me who I would be wrestling. His name was Duane Olson from Iowa State. He was a sophomore, and his college record was 16 wins and 2 losses. He only lost one match in high school. I didn't lose any matches in high school, of course, because I didn't have any matches in high school.

The next morning, I went to the gym to weigh in and then to attend a fifteen-minute meeting about freestyle rules. I had to wait two hours until my match with Duane Olson, which seemed like an eternity. In freestyle, you wrestle three periods that are three minutes long, and you start each period standing. At least I knew the referee, who was the Athletic Director at Eastern Montana College.

I shook hands with Duane. The whistle blew. Duane Olson disappeared. A split second ago, he was right in front of me. Oh no, my body was hoisted into the air, turned and slammed into the mat face first. It's called a souffle, and it's a really cool wrestling move if it's done to someone else. The next two minutes and fifty seconds, I was rolled, gut-wrenched and some other nasty stuff I didn't have a clue about, except my referee friend kept adding up the score. I heard, one, two, three and so on. Finally, the towel was thrown in to stop the madness.

Not only was I getting pummeled score-wise, but Duane head-butted me and gave me a cross-face that felt like he caved in my face. I managed to catch my breath and get to the center of the mat to start the second period. Because I was embarrassed and bruised, I said to Duane: "You might beat me, but you will never pin me!" Duane said: "I didn't want to pin you." In other words, he was just going to torture me for another six minutes. My referee friend said: "Ken, you're in for a long, long six minutes."

During the second period, I managed to stay close to the mat enough that Duane scored only a few points. I felt like I was going to puke. The third period was much the same until about 90 seconds to go, when I felt Duane get up high on me. He's trying to pin me, the rascal. I reversed him and scored two points. With about fifteen seconds to go, I got an escape and lo and behold, scored another point. Final score was 23 to 3. I was so close to winning – not!

Like the good sport that I am, I shook his hand and said to him: "If I had one more period, I think I could have beaten you." "Either you're a crazy man or you have one hell of a sense of humor." I visited with Duane later that evening and found out that he was a really nice young man. Thirteen months later, Duane was killed in a car accident. It broke my heart.

It was a double elimination tournament, so I wrestled a second match against a nineteen-year-old from Missoula. My friend also ref'd this match. I jumped out in front, 8 to 2 by the middle of the second period. I cradled him, arched my back and I could see his shoulders really close to being pinned when the ref slapped the mat. I jumped up elated that I get a win. My ref friend asked me: "Why are you so happy, you just pinned yourself." This ended a very brief, unsuccessful freestyle wrestling career.

I decided that being a 148-pounder sucked, so I proceeded to eat everything in sight. In eight months, I weighed 246 pounds, kidding myself that I wasn't really fat, because I was so solid. The only thing that was really solid on me was my cranium.

CHAPTER 11

There Is a Snake in My Dryer...

During the summers, I worked on and got my Master's Degree in school administration from Montana State University. Typically, I would study from two in the morning until six, sleep an hour, then go to my eight o'clock class. You're probably in disbelief, but I had all As and only one B. The B was from a visiting professor who was a former school counselor who didn't like administrators. Even though I aced all of his tests, I still got a B. He was never asked to come back to the MSU campus. Oh well.

I started applying to some smaller schools in Montana that needed a superintendent. One afternoon, I got a call from the chairman of the school board in Winnett, Montana, Rex Bohn. He said: "I'm calling you to offer you the job of superintendent for our school district." "Where is Winnett?" "It's about fifty miles east of Lewistown, which is the center of Montana. Our town, as of yesterday, has 213 people in it." "And there is only one grouch in the whole town." "Our county has only 630 folks." "It's the least populated county in all of the U.S.A." "We're sort of proud of that." "My second question is are you going to build an elementary school, a library and a gymnasium?" "We are." "Would I have any say in how they are designed?" "Absolutely, we want you to work with the architects to come up with a final design." "We'll send you around to different schools to pick out the best features that you think would work for us." "I'll take the job." I didn't ask what they wanted to pay me.

My job in Winnett started on July 1. By this time, I was married and had three daughters. I had a lot of stuff to move. I asked five of my drinking, powerlifting, hunting buddies if they would help me move. "Oh, hell yes" was the common answer. The only stipulation was that I had to buy their booze. I rented a big U-Haul truck, and they provided two big trucks and a trailer. We got busy and loaded everything into the trucks and the trailer with hardly any miscues. John Humble, one of my best and craziest friends said, "Let's all go downtown for a few drinks to celebrate you getting out of the prison city."

We agreed to meet at the Corner Bar around eight. We noticed that besides the usual locals, that there were a bunch of strangers in the bar, and they were mostly Mexicans. I know from picking potatoes when I was a kid that a lot of Mexicans came to the potato fields for seasonal work. Somewhere around midnight, with most of us in the tank, we mostly agreed that we should vamoose.

About the time we were getting ready to leave one of the potato pickers bumped into John Humble and told him "To get the f--- out of my way!" "No!!!!" I knew that this confrontation wasn't going to end well, especially for the Mexican. John picked him up off his feet and chucked him over the bar and into a bunch of bottles. In no time, another Alamo broke out. A chubby looking one, kind of reminded me of Pancho Villa, swung at my noggin. I ducked the punch and hit him in his bread basket. Wheezing, he was toast. I just didn't want him to puke on me. The next few minutes looked like Armageddon.

Luckily, someone called the police who were close by, which stopped a lot of bleeding. We promised to pay for all the damages, which amounted to $180. Our fivesome ended up with three black eyes, one broken nose, a cracked rib and a bunch of minor cuts and bruises. This would be a really long trip to Winnett.

I told my fighters that I wanted to leave by 9 A.M. Unbelievably, they all showed up on time, black eyes and all. We decided to drive straight through to Lewistown, about 220 road miles. We stopped at a drive-in to load up on burgers and fries. My pals stopped at a convenience store to buy two cases of beer. Hey, they can't get too far out of line in the next hour of driving to Winnett. What I didn't know was that they were drinking all the way to Lewistown.

We arrived in Winnett at four in the afternoon. Winnett is so small. The school district provided a house for the superintendent that was only a block away from the schools. We pulled up in front of the house, and the school's 83-year-old janitor, Ernie, was there waiting for us. I can't imagine what he was thinking when he got a gander at the motley crew, including his new superintendent. I suspect he thought, what have we got ourselves into, hiring this guy? I had a pretty good lump on my head from being smacked by one or more of the Alamo guys, but I looked way better than most of my helpers.

My crew's highest priority was to see how fast they could get my stuff into the house, so they could get back to Lewistown to continue partying. They formed a chain gang so they could start tossing TVs and furniture from one to another without much regard for the welfare of my furniture. It was a small miracle that any furniture made it into the house without being demolished.

I said my good-byes to my friends. I knew I was really going to miss those knot-heads. I said a little prayer for their safe arrival back to Deer Lodge. Thank the Lord, they all made it in one piece. On my first night in my new home, I had a tough time going to sleep because after ten o'clock, I could not hear a sound outside and my window was open. Surely, out of 231 residents, someone would be doing something that would make noise. But that was hardly ever the case. The most noise I ever heard was when the neighbor's cat went into heat.

Winnett sits down in a little basin. There is a small, slow-moving creek running along its southern perimeter. Its football field was across the street from my house. The second afternoon, Ernie the janitor drove up in his old truck and wanted to show me something in the back of his pickup. He proudly picked up a 6-foot rattlesnake. "I killed this one with a hoe, and got the other one in my pickup the same way. Both of 'em were crawling around the football field." "Ernie, I'm afraid of snakes, I hate them." "Oh boy, I'll try to herd them away from your house. Do you want me to put a screen over the dryer vent on the outside of your house?" "Why?" "Well, a snake went into the vent and ended up in the dryer. The last superintendent thought he would solve the problem by turning on the dryer. That really made that snake mad." I didn't want any more details. Maybe being superintendent here is not such a good idea. And then I thought maybe Ernie, after witnessing my arrival, had his way of encouraging me to get out of Dodge. In time, we became great friends.

What I soon found out about the Winnett school system was that there was a huge opportunity for improvement. Their football team had won only two games in two years. Their school colors were black and white. Instead of the Rams, they should have been nicknamed the convicts. They didn't have any bleachers or a track. I guess they weren't necessary because hardly anyone came to the games and very few students went out for track. They didn't have a band, and no one seemed to know the school song.

The elementary school was ancient and in shambles. The gym was tiny with hardly any seating. Weight training equipment was nowhere to be found. You get the picture. It wasn't pretty, but I thought, this is perfect. I was positive that I could make a positive difference in so many ways.

After meeting with the head football coach, I realized he was a very nice young man who didn't know squat about coaching football. I don't think he even played any football. I started to worry about what the rest of the faculty was like, and I was not optimistic.

My first meeting with the school board was a pleasant surprise. They were very committed to making their school district a lot better. I found out that these were men who kept their word and had a lot of common sense. The board was mostly made up of ranchers. During the first meeting, a date was set to try to pass a mill levy to fund the school building project. I crossed my fingers and hoped it would pass.

The election was held the first week in August. If it passed, a new elementary school, a library and a gymnasium would be built. When the day came for the vote to take place, I was one nervous rookie superintendent. I was determined to watch the vote from the opening at 8 A.M. until the close at 8 P.M. Oh, oh, I couldn't believe how old a lot of the voters were who came in and after a while, I thought there is no way for the levy to pass. What I didn't know was just how important the school was to these folks. The final vote came with 127 in favor and only 13 against the passage. Wow!! Bless their hearts. I vowed to work as hard as I possibly could to see that Winnett had a school system they could be proud of, because they deserved it. Hang on, change is about to happen.

The first change was easy. I added gold to the black and white school colors. Because they didn't know or really didn't have a school song, I got the board to accept the Notre Dame fight song as their school song. I'm a lifelong Irish fan. Next, I had a meeting with all of the boys who wanted to play football. I suggested that they must go out for track if they were serious about winning football games. Some of these guys didn't even know how to run properly. I'm not kidding. They sort of waddled rather than run. Also, I wanted them to start lifting weights year around, even through the summer. Amazingly, this super bunch totally bought into everything I suggested.

My wonderful old janitor, after I told him I wanted to build some bleachers, said he knew about a bunch of abandoned 2" pipe that was left in the Flat Creek oil field just thirty miles south of Winnett. "They would be for the taking." "I'll teach you how to weld so we can make the bleachers ourselves." We decided that we would build enough bleachers that would seat 600 fans. Pretty darn optimistic considering there were only 630 people in the entire county. I was sure if we started winning, fans would come in from the surrounding area to watch the games. When some of the citizens of Winnett saw what we were doing, all of a sudden we had a bunch of lumber for the seats. Also, a lot of donated help putting the finishing touches on the project. The following year, we filled the bleachers with fans. How about that!

Nosing around the old elementary building, I found a room that had a bunch of old band equipment stored in it. At the next board meeting, I asked if it would be OK to start a band. "We don't have to buy anything, the instruments and uniforms are ready to go." The next day, one of the board members called me and said one of his rancher friend's wives was a music major. I called her and asked her if she would like to be our band director. She didn't hesitate and said she would like to give it a go. The first year, starting a band was an exercise in patience for all of us within hearing distance. The second year, the band performance was almost bearable and worth every minute.

The first week of school everything seemed to be under control until Thursday around noon. I was looking out of my office window watching the grade school playground. At first, I couldn't believe what I was seeing. One of the high school boys was trying to light a tiny first-grader's dress on fire. I raised my office window as high as it would go and dove through the opening, landing on my hands and knees. I ran over to the little girl to make sure her dress wasn't burning and that she was OK. Out of the corner of my eye, I saw the pervert running toward the street. He jumped over the fence, and I was in hot pursuit. Trying to jump over the fence, I caught my foot on the top wire and landed in a heap, ripping my pants and tearing my sport coat. I was livid.

From the school grounds, it's about a half mile uphill to the highway where my red-headed Firestarter was heading as fast as his legs would carry him. Getting to the top of the hill, he turned east and ran down the highway toward where his home was, I guess. The last thing I wanted was for him to get away from me, but try as I might, I couldn't gain on him. I chased him for about four miles before he turned off the highway and started running up a gravel road without any sign of slowing down. I'm not going to tell you what I yelled at him. I walked home disgusted and angry at myself for not being able to keep up with the varmint. It was probably best for both of us that I couldn't catch him. The next morning, the step-dad of the fire bug came into my office mad as hell. He was stammering and sputtering. I told him to settle down and be quiet until I let him know what Jimmy tried to do. Also, I told him that I think his stepson needs psychological help because a normal teenager would never even think of setting a little girl's dress on fire.

"Jimmy is not to come back to school until he gets well, because he is sick. Come to the next school board meeting if you want to challenge my decision." Stepdad never came to the school board meeting. His stepson never came back to Winnett High School. I found out later that Jimmy, last year, snuck into the boys' locker room and took a dump into one of the football player's duffel bag. He pooped into the wrong bag because the football player found him and kicked the snot out of him. Thank the good lord, Jimmy was the total exception to the rule. The rest of the kids in school were wonderful.

We did have one other problem I had to quickly take care of. I found out that there were three dropouts hanging around the school during the noon hour and after school. They were suspected of selling drugs. I spotted them across the street from the school, so I went over and had a short visit with them. I wasn't at all cordial. They never came back.

We bussed kids in from as far away as sixty-four miles one way. That long, long trip went down into the Musselshell River country. The last sixteen miles was over gumbo roads. If you never experienced gumbo roads, when it gets wet, it sticks to everything like super-glue, including tires. We picked up some of these students in the dark and in the wintertime, they didn't get home until it was dark again. They hardly ever missed school.

I would meet the buses coming in before school to make sure there were no problems on the routes. I noticed that when I went into the school, most of the students would follow me in. I met with the faculty and suggested to them that I didn't think we needed to ring bells anymore. Each teacher had a period assigned to them and when the hour was up, they would dismiss their students. When the rest of the high school students heard the noise of dismissed students, they would be dismissed and were expected to walk directly to their next class. It worked. Instead of goofing around and just getting to their next class in the nick of time, they just walked to the next class. It saved a bunch of time. The students felt like we trusted them to do the right thing. Fellow administrators told me I was crazy, and you have to ring bells because that's the way it's always been. They were wrong.

The Winnett students were exceptionally responsible and mature. Mostly, farm and ranch kids knew how to work and take care of things. If they didn't behave in school, they were in big trouble at home. An example, on the second day of school, the Brady twins, two junior boys, came into my office and asked me if I wanted them to change the flat tire on my car. They did. How nice. The little snots at White Sulphur Springs would have let the air out of all of my tires.

Talking with the seniors the next year, I found out that most of them had never been out of the state of Montana and some thought Billings was as big as New York or Chicago. No kidding! I asked all of the senior parents to come into school and meet with me just before Christmas vacation. I asked for volunteers who would be willing to take the seniors on a trip to Las Vegas, then to California, up the coast to Sacramento and then return home to Winnett. Four parents volunteered to make the trip. All of them had camper trailers and so did I. You can't imagine how excited the seniors were to see the sights in Nevada and California. We had ourselves a little convoy.

Every night when we arrived at our camping spots, the seniors would set up the trailers and get everything ready to stay overnight without being asked. When we got to Las Vegas, I wanted them to see the famous Las Vegas strip. Before we started walking past the casinos, I gathered the seniors around me and told them to stay close behind me, to avoid any trouble. When I stopped at the first stop light, seventeen bodies bumped into me. They weren't about to let me get out of their sight. They were wide-eyed, looking at some of the strange creatures that you can encounter on the strip.

During the entire trip, we didn't have one problem with the students. It was fun to see how excited they were to experience things that were so new to them. Maybe the most memorable event was our stay in Sacramento. One of our parents was a good friend of the lead detective on the Zodiac Killer case. We stayed overnight on the detective's property. That evening, after dinner, he sat down with the seniors and told them as much as he could about the case. He sure had their total attention as well as mine. I just knew that this trip would be a special memory for the rest of the seniors' lives.

I had so much trust in the senior class that I set up a unique program for their last quarter of high school. Typically, seniors spend their last quarter hardly learning anything. I wanted to change that. We asked the seniors what they wanted to do for a living after high school. Two of the boys thought they would like to be veterinarians. We had them intern with a veterinarian in Roundup. Another wanted to be a carpenter. We found a construction company that was willing to teach him the basics. A young lady thought she would like to go into nursing. She was welcomed to be a volunteer at the hospital in Lewistown. Parents either drove them to their work sites or they drove themselves. I know what you're probably thinking. That I opened myself and the school district to potential liability issues. You would be correct. We did have the parents sign waiver of liability forms. I simply wasn't that concerned because of my trust in the seniors. Every Monday, all of the seniors had to come to school to work with their assigned teacher who monitored their progress. Also, they were required to write an extensive term paper detailing their work assignment.

One of the boys who thought he wanted to be a vet actually became one, and the other boy soon found out that he didn't want any part of what was required. That was a win for both boys. The young lady who wanted to be a nurse became one and went on to work in a hospital in Billings. I submitted an overview of the program to the state education department. I was told that several small rural schools adopted a similar program around the country. I was forever grateful to the Winnett School Board members for having the courage and foresight to approve this program. Bless their hearts.

CHAPTER 12

Working Out with Clint Eastwood

I soon found out that the Winnett boys really did want to become winners. They religiously lifted weights year-round. Almost all of them went out for track. The Brady boys ran into town from their ranch to lift weights in the summer, which was a round trip of fourteen miles. That's dedication. The head football coach was a nice guy who didn't know anything about football, so I was lucky to find an assistant coach who knew a lot about the game. He was very good at teaching technique and fundamentals. The head coach gave pretty darn good pep talks. I also helped coach and it was really cool to see the improvement in our team. The opposing teams were going to be in for a bunch of surprises.

Luckily, a family from California moved in to run a truck stop and café at the top of the hill by the highway. Their son was a junior and a very good quarterback who was an excellent runner as well as a passer. He was just what we needed!

So, with new uniforms, with gold added to the black and white, new bleachers, and the start of a band and some pretty fair coaching, the Rams went five and four. Their dedication to weight training and turning out for track paid off big time. The next year, they were eight and one, winning the conference title. They ended up third in the division in track and had a state champion in the discus. I coached the state discus champion, and he won despite my help.

During my two-year stay in Winnett, a beautiful elementary school, library and gymnasium were built. I taught three classes a day and was substitute bus driver. To raise money for the athletic program, I organized a boxing smoker. The word got out quickly and I was paid a visit by the Matovich brothers, who lived at the end of the Musselshell River, next to Fort Peck Reservoir. They didn't have electricity until the 1950s. Both of them were Golden Glove boxing champions in New York before they moved west. In my day, I've run into a lot of really tough hombres, but these two put all of them to shame. They wanted to help with the boxing matches. Great! I asked them to train the boys, and also to referee the matches. The gym was absolutely packed. The boys fought as hard as they could and even better, no one got seriously hurt. Thank the good lord the Matovich brothers liked me. Their way of greeting you was to slug you in the shoulder and just about knock you off your feet. I can't imagine what would happen to you if they didn't like you. I'm glad I never found out.

All of my life, I've loved sports, so when I found out that a sporting goods store in Lewistown was for sale, I thought I had better look into the possibility of buying it. It would be a stretch, as I hadn't saved any money. The sporting goods store was called E'Jays. It was owned by a little Jewish fellow, Leon Jacobs, who I soon found out was quite a character. Don't ask me how, but I managed to borrow one hundred and eighty thousand dollars from a local bank in Lewistown. I found out later that a couple of Winnett School Board members went to bat for me. The store sold athletic equipment to schools in four states. I didn't have a clue what I just got myself into. Little did I know that more than half of the inventory was outdated. Also, the guy in charge of shipping had been stealing from Leon for over two years. Leon knew it, but didn't have the heart to fire the guy. I wish Leon had called him out and paid him a decent wage, so he didn't have to be a crook to get by. Later, it became clear to me that one of the secretaries was dipping into the cash register on a regular basis. I was starting in a very deep hole that maybe I couldn't climb out of.

Selling sporting goods was easy for me, and I went after it like Grant taking Vicksburg. In the first year, I doubled the gross sales. That was really a good idea, right? Wrong! What I found out was that schools were really slow payers, and the suppliers were quick on billing, so without enough working capital, I found myself in a financial mess. To make matters worse, I met two nice young accountants in Billings who wanted to buy a portion of the business and bring their financial expertise and also inject working capital into the business. In less than six months, they stole about three hundred thousand dollars out of the business. I should have sued them, but for what? I just wanted them out of my life. I have a saying that time wounds all heels, and I'm sure they met with some hard times.

I've never regretted buying the sporting goods store, even though it just about buried me in more ways than one. Because I was an avid weightlifter, I could easily sell coaches on the benefits of weight training. I began selling sixteen- station Universal gyms. The first one

I sold was to a school in Worland, Wyoming. I hauled it down with my pickup, pulling a trailer with all the parts in it. My helper was a seventy-year-old man who was a great guy but didn't have a lot of mechanical skill. We hauled all the weight stacks and well over a hundred parts into a room next to the gymnasium where they wanted the Universal gym set up. My partner and I were staring at the pile of parts not knowing where to start. A coach asked if we needed any help. "Yep, we need a lot of help." He said, "There's a seventh-grader who is really good at this sort of thing. I'll go get him." Soon, this little guy appeared. He looked over everything for a few minutes and then said: "You need to set-up the base first and then put those four metal parts onto each corner." That little bugger was a life saver. If he didn't help us, we would probably still be in Worland. I gave him fifty bucks. It was money well spent.

I could sell Universal gyms like hotcakes. In the next year, we installed forty-four gyms. I think we set a record by setting up eight, sixteen-station machines in two and one-half days. I had a friend who owned a semi that could haul eight gyms. He was a big old ex-basketball player for the University of Montana. As the saying goes, he could eat hay off the top of the stack. He was at least 6'7" tall and weighed about 280 pounds. His name was Steve Lowery. Steve would drive up to the eight school gyms and drop off the machine as close as he could get to their final destination.

The former owner of EJ's, Leon Jacobs, owned a Mooney airplane, a three-seater. Leon would fly Mel, my old helper, and me to each of the little town's airports and we would call ahead to have a coach pick us up and drive us to the gyms. By this time, Mel and I could set up a gym in two hours or less. As soon as they were set up, off we went to the next town. The last gyms were set up at about ten at night. Then we would hit the hay and do the same process for the next day and a half. Actually, we had a blast setting up the machines. The last night in the motel after we had a couple of beers, Leon, all 5'2" of him, and Mel, 140 pounds soaking wet, decided they could take me down and pin me. I was laughing so hard, they had a chance of succeeding. Thank the good lord neither one had a heart attack.

Because of my commitment to selling Universal gyms, and the number of sales I made, which was a per capita for them, I was offered a factory representation and/or Universal Gym job. At the time, I didn't know that this would become one of the highlights of my life. Every August, Universal set up a display of their newest 16-station gym at the coaches' clinic held in Great Falls, Montana. Over 1200 coaches and athletic directors attended the clinic. The event was always held at the Heritage Inn, the nicest and largest motel in Great Falls. I was to assist Chuck Coker, who was the star attraction, at the event. Chuck was an All-American football player at Stanford University. At 6'3" and 240 pounds, he was one of the most impressive people I have ever met. I soon idolized the guy. He was ruggedly handsome. Everywhere he went, women would stare at him.

At the first session, Chuck had an audience of about 700 coaches. We had the newest Universal Gym all set-up and ready to go. Pretty exciting for me. Chuck started off by saying, "I wouldn't want most of you coaching my son." That got their full attention. He continued, "Most of you are overweight and out of shape. You are poor examples for your athletes to look up to." Then, he took off his shirt. Holy cow, was he ever put together! Then he said, "If any one of you can do what I'm about to do, I'll give this Universal Gym to your school free of charge." "Ken, put the bench press pin into the bottom of the stack at 320 pounds." He started doing reps while talking to the coaches. I counted over sixty reps and he didn't look even a little bit tired. Chuck was fifty-six years old at the time. You could hear a pin drop out in the audience. He had their undivided attention.

After we finished demonstrating for the day, Chuck asked me if I wanted to wait around and work-out with a friend of his around five. "Sure, I want to work out anyway." After waiting a little while, the back door opened and in walked none other than Clint Eastwood. I looked at Chuck in disbelief. "Clint's a friend of mine and he wants to work out and try the new machine. You don't mind?" Wow, what a cool surprise! Clint worked out really hard and had a ton of questions, mainly for Chuck. When we finished up, he asked us if we wanted to meet him for dinner. Alright! Clint asked me if I drank beer. "I do." "Good, Chuck doesn't drink, and I want to have a beer or two with you and find out everything you know about Montana." We agreed to meet at the far end of the restaurant bar so he wouldn't be noticed so much. Clint was filming "Thunderbolt and Lightfoot" just outside of Great Falls, and that was why he was staying at the Heritage Inn.

We sat in the back of the restaurant and Clint ordered a couple of beers. This will be my chance to show him what a real beer-drinking Montanan is like. He finished his first beer in just short of record time and promptly ordered two more. It worked out for both of us because he finished off the next two before I was done with beer number one. I was out of my league. On top of that, he never showed any signs of being tipsy, not even close. What fun he was, and he really did want to know everything about Montana history. Luckily, I'm a Fourth Generation Montanan, and could do a pretty fair job of telling stories about our great state. Clint was one of the most enjoyable men I've ever known. We met for dinner and beers the next three evenings.

Chuck's practice was to get up at 4:30 and run three or four miles. The first morning, he was joined by about 100 coaches whom he shamed into trying to get into shape in order to set a good example for their athletes. A lot of the coaches were really hurting after trying to keep up with Chuck, including myself. The second morning, about half of the coaches failed to make the 4:30 starting time. The third morning, only six showed up. So much for good intentions.

Some of my buddies wanted me to go out on the town with them, but I said I was going to hang out with Clint Eastwood. One of them said, "Sure, and I'm Mother Theresa." The look on their faces was priceless when they saw me walking into the Heritage Restaurant with him. Clint ended up buying two Universal gyms. He sure gave me something to tell my grandkids years later.

Soon after the Great Falls clinic, I flew to Anaheim, California, for the National Sporting Goods Convention to help out at the Universal Gym booth. In the second hour, I was demonstrating bench presses on the Universal Gym. I was doing the entire stack which was 325 pounds. When I was finished, I looked up and saw Kenny Norton, the heavy weight boxing champion of the world looking at me. "Can I give it a try?" "Sure, have at it." Kenny Norton was one big dude. He got into position and pushed as hard as he could, but the weight didn't move. He stood up and, looking down at me said, "how can a little guy like you easily lift that much and I can't." I asked him to lift his arms and hold them out in front of him. Then I put up my short arms next to his. His arms were at least a foot longer than mine. "It's leverage. I have a mechanical advantage, being short-armed." I could immediately see the relief on his face. He said, "so that's it, I thought there was something seriously wrong with me." We visited for a while and he was a real gentleman, thank goodness.

The next Universal event I attended was held in West Yellowstone, Montana. The event taking place was the National Conference for weight trainers. All of the big hitters in the weight-lifting field were in attendance. The vast majority of attendees were strong advocates of free-weight-lifting and were not fond of stationary gyms such as our Universal Gym. I certainly wasn't the main representative for Universal, Ed Burke was the man. Ed was a world class hammer thrower who represented the USA in the Olympics. At 6'5" and 265 pounds, Ed was a very impressive physical specimen. He also was one of the finest people I have ever met. Like Chuck Coker, he was very softspoken, but had a presence that commanded your attention and respect. Ed was able to convince most in attendance that stationary gyms had a valuable place in the weight training arena.

Several years later, Ed showed up at the coaches' clinic in Great Falls. I hardly recognized him. He was pale, gaunt and weighed no more than one hundred and seventy pounds. I asked him if he had been sick. "No. I guess you don't know what happened." "What happened?" He told me his wife and little daughter were in their car watching Ed practice throwing the hammer. "I released the hammer early and it flew into the windshield and the glass shattered and cut my wife's face, but thank God missed my little daughter." Ed told me he just didn't have the heart to work out anymore. I asked Ed if his wife wanted him to continue throwing the hammer. "She does." "I'll bet she would like to have the old Ed back." With the encouragement of his many friends, Ed began to work out again and qualified for the next

Olympics. Because of his courage, his fellow Olympians chose him to carry in the U.S. flag during the Opening Ceremony. Watching Ed on T.V., I cried with happiness for Ed and his family. A moment I'll never forget.

I was offered a full-time job with Universal Gym, which I would have loved, but with three little daughters, I just couldn't justify being away from them so much. It was a very dark time in my life as I had to liquidate the sporting goods business to pay off the creditors. I met with the banker who loaned me the money to buy E'Jays and he said I had to declare bankruptcy. There was no other way. I said, "I'm not sure who was dumber, me for borrowing so much without any working capital, or you for loaning it to me. Also, I'm not declaring bankruptcy no matter what. My dad would disown me." I decided to liquidate as much inventory as I could.

Some of my Catholic friends told the head Pastor at St. Leo's Parish that I was selling or getting out of the sporting goods business. He approached me after mass and said that the Good Lord wanted me to be Superintendent of Schools as well as be Parish Administrator. I could have easily said no to Father Flanagan, but saying no to the Good Lord was an entirely different matter.

CHAPTER 13

My Fifty Pound Hero Davey Farber

In order to please the Good Lord and because I needed the money, I accepted Father Flanagan's offer to become Superintendent of the St. Leo's schools. The job consisted of supervising the schools and raising money to keep the schools open. A major goal was to increase enrollment. St. Leo's had an incredible athletic program in the past, especially in football. In recent years, it had fallen on hard times. I thought I knew what to do to turn it around.

During the summer, I hired a hard-nosed football coach who could really coach, but was a little rough around the edges. An occasional F-bomb would fly out of his mouth making the nuns and priests cringe a little bit.

Similar to my experience in Winnett, I could help do stuff that was not in an average superintendent's job description. St. Leo's had a dilapidated elementary building that had to be torn down. For a month in the summer, I ran a jack hammer to knock holes into the cement basement. I'm pretty good at no-brainer work if I do say so myself. The next part of this book is far and away more important and meaningful than all of the rest of it put together. If you do nothing else, please remember Davey Farber. Here's why.

On the first day of school at St. Leo's, I was walking down the hallway to my office when I saw what looked like a 3rd or 4th grader standing by my office. He was a cute little guy who looked very, very frail and I guessed he weighed no more than fifty pounds. He had long blond hair and light blue eyes. I asked him the obvious question: "Why aren't you in school?" "I want to go to school, but I don't want to be put in the fourth grade. I want to be in the eighth grade." "How old are you?" "I'm fourteen. I have cystic fibrosis and because my lungs fill up with fluid, I can't stay in school for a full day because I start coughing and I get sent home. So, they keep me in the fourth grade. I've been in the fourth grade for the last three years. I'm really smart and if you would let me be in the eighth grade, I promise you I won't die until I graduate." "So, you give me your word you won't die until after you graduate?" "Yes sir, I sure do." I called my secretary over and told her to get David his eighth-grade books and walk him over to the eighth-grade class and introduce him to his new classmates. David had a big smile on his face.

I thought I had better not get too attached to this little guy because when he dies, it will probably break my heart. For the first few days, I would check in on David to see how he was doing. Try as he might, he just couldn't last a full day and his mom would be called from work to pick him up. I thought it wouldn't hurt for me to give him a ride home. Looking back, those little rides gave my life a real purpose.

Just about every morning, I would meet with a bunch of my softball and hunting buddies to have breakfast as the Snow White Café, which was only two blocks from St. Leo's. I asked them if it would be O.K. to bring David to have breakfast with them. I told them why it was so important. Bless their hearts, it was a unanimous yes! It was so important for David to have some nice men in his life as his father couldn't deal with David's illness and had abandoned his family. David told me that his older brother died of the same illness when he was sixteen. David's dad apparently couldn't handle a second son's death. Our breakfast bunch started out with three or four of us and ended up with over a dozen because of David. He did a lot of giggling listening to my friend's stories and jokes.

The entire climate of the school changed because of David. To watch this little guy desperately trying to make it through the school day inspired every student to try harder to do their best in school. They watched him in gym class, and because he couldn't run without coughing, he decided to try to make a free throw. He just didn't have enough strength to get the ball to the basket. Nevertheless, he just kept trying over and over. I found out what he was trying to do, so I went to my failing sporting goods store and got him a much smaller ball. It didn't take him very long until he could make a basket. When he made the first one, the kids told me he was so happy that it was like he won the NCAA national basketball championship.

When David felt well enough, he wanted to attend football and basketball games. During football season, St. Leo's had an out-of-town game with Denton, a small farming community located about thirty miles north of Lewistown. There is a house in Lewistown that is said to be the actual center of Montana. I asked David if he wanted to go. He did. On the back road to Denton, there is hardly any traffic. About halfway to Denton, I asked David if there was anything he wanted to do before he died. "Sure, I always wanted to drive a car." "Well, well, now is your chance to drive." I pulled my big old Cadillac over to the side of the road and parked. "Are you ready to drive?" I'll never forget his answer. "I know I'm going to die pretty soon, but I'm not sure you want to die with me driving your car." "Slide over into the driver's seat – I'll take my chances." Thank goodness the old Cadillac was an automatic, not a straight stick, giving David a chance to drive it. He could barely see over the steering wheel. He creeped along slowly but was thrilled to be herding the old car up the road.

After Davey seemed satisfied with his driving opportunity, I took over and drove into Denton. I parked in front of a bar restaurant that I frequented several times when I was chasing pheasants around the grain fields outside of town. I knew the bartender pretty well. David had told me another thing he wanted to do was to taste a little whiskey because his dad drank a ton of it before he vanished, and Davey wanted to know why he liked it so much. I asked the bartender to give my little buddy a small shot of whiskey. "What, are you nuts? I can't serve a little boy whiskey." "Look, this young man is dying from cystic fibrosis, his lungs are filling up and he will soon be gone. So, it sure as hell can't hurt him and it's not going to be the reason he dies." "Ok, ok, I suppose it will be alright." David took a tiny sip and spit it out. "Why would anyone like to drink that stuff? It tastes like gasoline." "So, you know what gasoline tastes like?" "I'm just guessing." We ate a little lunch and off we went to the football game. I drove. Sadly, I had to take him home at halftime because he started coughing. It still was one of the best days of my life and I know it was also one of David's.

As the school year went on, Davey became weaker and weaker. In one of our visits, I asked him what he regretted most about being so sick. "The only thing I can think of is when you and your breakfast friends made me laugh, a lot of times it made me start coughing. Other than that, I really can't think of anything else." If I had his illness, my list of complaints would have been a mile long.

With two weeks to go before graduation, David had to be hospitalized because he could barely breathe. He was in a great deal of pain. I went to the hospital to visit him. Looking into his room, I saw my physical therapist friend pounding him on the chest so hard, I thought he would break his ribs. I grabbed him and pulled him away from David. I said, "Stop hitting so hard, I won't stand for it." He told me if he didn't dislodge some of the fluid build-up, he would die tonight.

I tried to talk to Davey after the pounding stopped, but I could hardly hear him. He still had a little smile on his face. I told him that I expected him to keep his promise to show up for graduation. He whispered that he would be there. On the way home, I had trouble driving, I was crying so hard. I don't pray enough, that's for sure, but that night I prayed for David's pain to go away. I didn't think he had any chance of getting out of the hospital.

I went to the hospital every chance I got to check in on Davey. Sometimes, he was asleep and sometimes he was too weak to talk. His mom kept me updated every day on how he was doing.

Eighth grade graduation was on Saturday evening at 7 P.M. in the church. Because I was superintendent, I was asked to give the commencement address and to hand out the diplomas. I told the priest who was saying mass that I hoped David would show up. He said:

"I don't think that will happen." At seven, the church was filled with parents and friends of the graduates, but no David. The priest wanted to start, but I told him to wait and that I wasn't going to start without Davey and if he doesn't show, I can't do my part of the ceremony. I thought he might have a coronary. We waited and waited for what seemed an eternity with everyone looking at me like I didn't know what time it was. I said, "I'm waiting for David Farber to be here for graduation." I kept staring at the front door. At seven minutes after seven, the front door slowly opened. I couldn't believe my eyes. Davey was being carried in by his mother.

What happened next, I couldn't talk about for several years without choking up. David's mom carried him up to the alter where I was standing. I leaned over to greet him. Davey put his tiny arms around my neck and said, "I love you." I barely remember the rest of the ceremony.

David's mom wrote a poem about his graduation ceremony. I have included it at the end of this chapter. Davey's mom won't get an award for poetic proficiency, but it is the most inspirational and meaningful poem I have ever read.

Graduation Day

May twenty-sixth 1978 –
graduation day. A day
we've all waited for – in
a way it means no more
silly fun, our babyish
days are over and done.
We are growing teenagers–
each and everyone. The
procession has started –
shall we run? "No, let's
begin our march up the
aisle." Two-by-two, not
in single file. Twenty-
four of us, oh how neat,
our class can't be beat.
The Mass begins, everyone
is quiet... we made it to
our seats without a riot...
Our parents are seated,
pleased as punch. They're
probably all thinking,
"what a super bunch." It's
time for our diploma and
the superintendent stands,
if it wasn't in church,
we'd all clap our hands.
But the first thing he
said as he stood during
Mass, "I'd like to present
an honorary diploma to
a member of the class. A
little boy who's done so
much for everyone in our
school. He's a perfect
example of the golden
rule." The little boy
walked till he reached
the outstretched arm. He
received his diploma from
the man–tender and
warm. He embraced that
little boy with a tear
in his eye and there
wasn't a person in Church
who wasn't asking God
why? Oh why? God, let
us pray on our graduation
day, make this little boy
well, we'll do anything
you say. He has given so
much with tender little
smiles. Oh God, let him
stay with us for a long,
long while. We've all
grown up a little bit
tonight and I know
everything will be al-
right. That little boy
turned and his eyes filled
with tears and God talk-
ed to us and lifted all
our fears. God put this
little boy in our class
for a reason, it's as plain
as day and night, plain
as every season. And
then I heard the super-
intendent say Kelly,
Betty, Kevan, Randy, Tim-
othy, Laura, Cari, Rick,
Annette, Marcia, Jeffrey,
Cecelia, Paul, Mary, Karen,
Theodore, Melinda, Steph-
en, Helen, Renee, Deborah,
Donna, Timothy, Ann, and
most of all, David.

Obituary from the Billings Gazette

Lewistown Graduate Succumbs

Fifteen-year-old David Farber didn't get to read about his 8th-Grade graduation in Wednesday's Gazette.

David, who missed most of the school year because he suffered from cystic fibrosis, joined his classmates at St. Leo's in Lewistown last week to receive his diploma. But, following the ceremony, he was hospitalized with pneumonia.

David had saved up his energy to accept his honorary diploma and it was one of the biggest days in the teenager's life.

A Gazette article had described his graduation day in Wednesday's edition, but late Tuesday night, David passed away.

'He made all of us forget our problems, as he faced probably the biggest problem anyone could', said Ken Colbo, school superintendent. 'He did so with courage, and never allowed anyone to feel sorry for him'.

Maryilynn Butenhoff, school secretary, visited David in the intensive care unit of the hospital not long after graduation, and she asked if there was anything he wanted.

David lifted his steam and oxygen mask, she said, and replied, 'Mrs. B., I'd like two Heath bars and some jellybeans to give to the kids when they come to see me.'

My second year and final year at St. Leo's went fairly well, with a couple of notable exceptions. I was told to hire the best sixth-grade teacher I could find. I did that. She was Mormon. When Father Flanagan found out, he roared into my office using the Good Lord's name in vain in referring to my selection. Before I threw him out of my office for swearing at me, I let him know that the three priests in the parish never taught one class at St. Leo's. In fact, they actually wanted the school to close because it was extra work for them to raise funds to keep it going. I had the last laugh because my sixth-grade teacher was so good that they hired her husband to teach in the high school and to coach football and basketball. So there you go!!

The other exception was that, as Parish Administrator, I decided to put the priests on a food budget. Two of the three priests were fat, and their alcohol consumption was out of control. Telling them that they had to stay within the budget went over like a lead balloon. I really didn't care that they were upset, because they weren't helping me keep the schools open.

CHAPTER 14

Hellgate High School ... Yes, That's Its Actual Name.

At the end of my second and final year at St. Leo's, I got a call from Dick Correll, who remembered me from applying for his football coaching job at Roundup High School. Dick was Principal at Hellgate High School. He said: "Hey Ken, I'm looking to hire an assistant principal at Hellgate. You need to know that it's the worst job in all of education. We have over two thousand students and room for only 1200. So, we have an open campus with no study halls. We have a nine-period day and students are only required to attend five periods. Because we don't know if students are supposed to be in class or if they have a free period, we have no clue if they are skipping class or not. What's really bad is that there can be as many as two hundred people hanging around the school that aren't students. They just want to cause problems and, in many cases, sell drugs. Teachers won't walk through the cafeteria because kids might throw food at them. It's so bad that some teachers are afraid to come out of their rooms between classes. Students frequently use the F word and God only knows what they have in their lockers. They pull fire alarms at least once a day. Last year, a student punched me in the nose and broke it. They varnished my truck last fall, so when I came out to go home, there were hundreds of leaves stuck to the truck. Finally, they smoke anywhere they want outside the building, but a lot of them smoke in the restrooms. They almost plugged up the drinking fountains by spitting snuff into them. There is more but I think you get the picture."

He continued: "I needed to tell you all of these things because I think this is the perfect job for you." "What?? Why?" "Well, I checked around and if you think you're right, you will stand up to anyone. Anyone who has the guts to hire a Mormon to teach in a Catholic school has to be crazy or thought it was the right thing to do. What do you say?" My response: "It sounds perfect. At least I can't mess it up much more than it already is. I can't wait to get to Missoula. Thank you."

My first meaningful assignment was to get the seniors registered for classes. Seniors were first to register, and they wanted to get to their counselors as soon as they could because they wanted their classes scheduled for the first five periods of the day. If they could do so, they would be finished with school by one o'clock and then they could goof around or they could get a part-time job. I was to let the seniors in one at a time and keep them in order. Picture five hundred seventeen-and-eighteen-year-olds all trying to squeeze through a three-foot opening. The nearest senior tried to push me aside. I stepped in front of him and blocked his way in. He said: "What the fuck? Let me in!" Oh man, this is going to be a lot of fun I thought. I told him: "You're not coming in today and also you are suspended for three days for swearing." "You can't suspend me; school hasn't even started." "How in the world did you get to be a senior? You are suspended when school starts." My voice is pretty loud so most of the seniors heard what I said. The next senior in line, a rather large boy said: "What the fuck is going on, you can't do that, man." "Well, now you're also suspended for three days." Now, I had their attention. "I will suspend any and all of you, if necessary, for swearing or for not showing proper respect for your teachers or administrators. The first senior I suspended said: "I want to see Correll." "There isn't a Correll here." "Like hell, he's standing right over there." "Oh, you mean Mr. Correll?" He wasn't happy about it, but he complied. I motioned for Dick to come over to visit with our little potty-mouths. Mr. Correll announced to the seniors that whatever I wanted to do, he would support me 100%, and if he decides to suspend all of you because you can't behave yourselves, then you can all go home without any classes being scheduled. Wow, he's going to back me, bless his heart. The seniors got the picture. I got a lot of strange looks, but I didn't hear another swear word. Off to a good start.

The first day of school, while walking down the hallway, I passed by two young ladies standing in front of their lockers. I could hardly believe what I saw! Their lockers were adorned with pictures of totally nude guys, full frontal. I told them to stay where they were, and I asked the nearest teacher to get my secretary. When she showed up at the lockers, I asked her to call the parents of the girls and have them come to school. I want them to see what their daughters have in their lockers. I stood there with the young ladies for at least an hour until their parents finally showed up. A long, long hour…

I asked the parents to look into the lockers and tell me if what you see is OK with them. Both sets of parents agreed that it was not

OK; in fact, it was disgusting. I said: "Take your daughter's home and visit with them about moral standards and what is not acceptable for sophomores in high school. They can come back to school, unless they think what they did was OK. Then, we have a real problem." It was quite amazing how many lockers were suddenly closed when I walked down the hallways.

Hellgate had a history of students pulling fire alarms and not being caught. Sometimes, as many as five would be pulled in one day. There was talk by the powers-that-be to just shut them off. "What? We cannot do that. This is an old building and what if there was a fire? I'll put an end to the fire alarm pulling". When I made that statement, I had no clue how I was going to stop the alarm pulling.

Most of the time, an alarm was being pulled on the first floor between first and second period. I went down to the first floor and looked around the area where the alarm was being pulled. I noticed that directly across from the fire alarm, there was a door that opened into a booth where tickets to plays were sold. A light bulb went off in my tiny brain. I went down to the janitor's area and found the head of maintenance eating a cinnamon roll, which wasn't an unusual practice for him. "Please send a janitor down to the ticket booth at 5:30 this afternoon. Tell him to bring a drill and some bits." I had the janitor drill a hole into the door so that I could see the alarm box by looking through the hole. Because some of the students arrived at school as early as six a.m., I had to get into the booth before 6. So, I sat in the dark waiting for the first period to end, so hopefully, I could catch the little varmint pulling the alarm. Sitting in the dark for three hours seemed like forever. I almost blew my cover because some boys came by and were trying to light the wooden edge of the booth on fire.

Damn, I wanted to open the door and nab them. I did hear two of their names, so I thought I could get them later. It's amazing what you hear when no one knows you are listening.

Finally, after what seemed an eternity, the bell rang ending first period. My heart rate went through the roof. I saw a hand go up to pull the alarm. Off it went. I threw the door open and leaped out of the booth. Damn, I couldn't see a thing! My vision was blurred from sitting in the dark for so long. I had no clue who the culprit was. Then, a senior boy, who I had suspended two weeks ago said: "He got on the first bus." At the time, we were bussing students to another location because we were so crowded. I thanked my new friend and quickly went over to the first bus. I climbed up the steps and stood at the front of the bus staring down the aisle. There were about thirty sets of eyes staring at me. Then, I saw one student who was almost on the floor. I went down the aisle, looked down at him and said "Got ya!" The little varmint was caught. He was expelled from school for a semester.

Like wildfire, the rumor went around the student body that I had drilled holes in almost every room, including the bathrooms. I did nothing to discourage those rumors. Very, very few fire alarms were pulled for the next eight years.

At the beginning of my third year at Hellgate, word got back to me that there was a fight involving four girls. Apparently, the fight took place under a bridge about a mile from Hellgate during the noon hour. Three Native American girls had to be admitted to the emergency room to get patched up from numerous cuts to their arms and faces. A sophomore girl had done all that damage all by herself. I found her and brought her to my office. Her name was Michelle. "What happened?" She said: "These Indians were calling me names and making fun of me." I expected her to be huge, but she wasn't. She was about 5'6" and around 140 pounds. I saw that she had rings on all of her fingers, and the knuckle rings had spikes on them. "They said I was a fat little bitch. I told them I would meet them under the bridge and fight all of them at the same time." My response: "So you cut them to ribbons and they had to be sent to the emergency room." "Damn right I did. Those bitches deserved it." "You have to go home and not come back to school until your parents come in to see me." "OK man, you're not going to want to talk to them, I'll guarantee that." "I'll take my chances." "Don't say I didn't warn you, they're mean as hell."

After walking the halls the next morning, I went to my office and was met by my secretary who looked like she just saw a ghost. "Michelle's parents are in your office and are mad as hornets. They are humungous and both are wearing truckers' jackets." "Thanks for the heads up."

Stepping into my office, I saw Mr. and Mrs. Truckers sitting in chairs across from my desk. My secretary wasn't kidding! They were huge. Both were over six feet tall and way over 250 pounds. They wore some pretty snazzy truckers' jackets, I must say. Being the friendly chap that I am, I said: "Hello, thanks for coming in to see me." They said nothing, but if looks could kill, I would be dead as a door nail. I sat down behind my desk. As soon as I got settled, Dad asked me if I knew what he liked to do on weekends. Trying my best to make him smile, I said: "I'll bet you like to play badminton." He didn't have a sense of humor. No hint of a smile. "I like to go downtown to the bars and beat the crap out of assholes like you." "Very interesting. What does that have to do with your daughter's suspension?" "If you don't put her back in school, you're going to find out." "I'll bet your daughter didn't tell you the truth about what happened." "You're calling her a liar?"

"Apparently, you're not interested in hearing the truth." "No!" "So you're going to kick my butt? Before, we start do you mind if I take my sport coat off because you will probably tear it into little pieces and I really like this sport coat." I took my time putting it on the coat rack. "Please let me take my tie off, I don't want you to grab it and slam my head into my desk." Again, I took a lot of time getting my tie off.

"I guess I am now ready to go. But, before we start, I want you to know that if you get really lucky and can beat me up, and trust me, you will have to be really, really lucky to get the job done, your daughter will still be suspended. By the way, nobody gets a pass on calling me an asshole. Now, get your fat ass up and let's get it done!"

He said: "What do you mean she will still be suspended?" "I'm going to tell you exactly what happened and don't interrupt me until I'm finished." After letting them know what took place, I just had to say: "Having listened to your nonsense, I can see why she has a terrible attitude. I want her back in school tomorrow, where she will be placed on in-school suspension for two weeks. If you look through the window behind you, you can see the room she will be in. I have teachers assigned to come in every period to help these kids with their homework. I use teachers who really care about the students at Hellgate. She has to complete her assignments, or she won't go back to regular classes. Finally, I'm going to assign the best counselor we have in the building to help her. I never give up on any student. Michelle has no chance to be a decent person unless you two change your behaviors. Lastly, I never want to see you in my office again."

I visited with Michelle several times in my office to see how she was doing. I found out that dear old Dad was her stepdad, not her real father. During one of our visits, she told me that her stepdad chased her around with a butcher knife, but he was too drunk to catch her. She acted like it was no big deal. I visited with all of her teachers to see if they could pay a little attention to her and cut her some slack, knowing that she was trying to just survive for another day. I wrote a letter to the so-called parents, letting them know that if I found out that they harmed her physically, I would turn them over to the authorities in a heartbeat. I sent copies to her counselor and the child welfare department.

While Michelle was on in-school suspension, our head basketball coach (Eric Hays) was assigned to watch her in seventh period. I saw him talking to Michelle and then giving her a book to read. After seventh period, I asked Michelle about the book. "Oh, Mr. Hays gave me a book he wants me to read. He said he wants to talk to me about one of the chapters on Thursday after school. Why would he do that? He's a big shot basketball coach." My response: "He must think you're worth talking to." "No way!" Thursday came and I watched Eric take Michelle aside after school and talk to her about the book. The next day, I asked Michelle about Eric's visit. "I don't get it, why would a big shot coach take time to talk to me?" "I already told you, he thinks you're worth talking to." For once, Michelle was speechless. She made it through her sophomore year without getting into any serious trouble at school. Her pathetic family moved out of state. I often think of her and wonder what happened to her. It's probably best I never found out. It was also probably best that Stepdad remained seated during his office visit.

I'm now going to tell you about the most horrible thing that happened while I was at Hellgate. It's probably the worst thing that will ever happen that was caused by a Hellgate student. It all started during noon hour. A teacher ran up to me in a panic. He said "I just saw a student drive his car over the curb and try to run over two Home EC teachers. They dove out of the way to keep from being run over." The teacher knew the student who was driving the car. He was a sophomore who had been in trouble before. His name was Jimmy Dixson. I found him in his English class and escorted him to my office.

I asked him point blank: "Did you try to run over the Home EC teachers?" He said, "I just bounced over the curb to scare them." "Why?" "I thought it would be fun." "You have got to be kidding me. Do you even know them?" "Nope." "So, you just wanted to scare or seriously hurt someone you don't even know?" "I guess so." "There's something seriously wrong with you and you cannot be in or near this school unless you get some help. I'm not a doctor, but I do know when someone is sick, and you are sick."

"Give me your car keys. You're going home. Where are your parents?" "I live with my mom. My asshole of a dad is long gone." "Is your mom home?" "She's on the road selling children's books. She's coming home tonight." "O.K. let's go, I'm taking you home." "You're actually going to take me home?" "Yes, you are not staying in this school for one second longer."

I gave Jimmy a ride home. On the way, he hardly said a word. I did tell him that it would probably be best if he just sat there and didn't say anything. He seemed more than OK with that. "Stay home until I can talk to your mother. If you don't, I'll have the police find you and lock you up." Jimmy said, "I do yard work for a judge who lives next door. Can I do that?" "Don't go any further than that."

After several tries, I finally reached his mother. I told her that she must be in my office at 8 A.M. and to make sure Jimmy stays home. She said she would be there. At ten minutes after eight, in she walked. She was a very small lady who looked to be in her late 40s. I didn't waste any time and told her what Jimmy did and why I took him home. I also said that I firmly believed that he needed serious mental help from a qualified professional. She said, "I think you are badly mistaken about my son. He is a very good boy and would never hurt anyone. He does yard work for the judge next door and I'm sure he would vouch for him." "I think he is the most dangerous boy I have ever met in my entire education career." "Nonsense." "Ok, let's do this. I'm going to bring a counselor in here and ask him who he thinks is the most dangerous student in this school and if he names your son, will you then listen to me?" "He won't name my son, but in the off chance he does, yes, I will listen to you."

I called one of the counselors and asked him to come into my office. When he arrived, I said to him: "You don't know this lady and I will introduce you to her after I ask you a very important question. It's very important that you give me an honest answer." "Of course I will." "Who would you consider to be the most dangerous student in this school?" Without hesitation, he answered "Jimmy Dixson." "I don't want to embarrass you, but this is Jimmy's mother." "Oh boy, I'm so sorry." "I would like to leave now." "Certainly." "So, Mrs. Dixson, will you listen to me now?" "I guess I must." "We, his counselor and I, recommend that Jimmy be put into St. Patrick Hospital for a mental evaluation." Ms. Dixson agreed to our recommendation.

On Tuesday night, Jimmy was sent to St. Patrick Hospital for his evaluation. He was released the following evening. On Friday, I received a call from Jimmy's mother saying: "I think we made a big mistake by sending Jimmy to St. Pats for the evaluation." "Why are you saying that?" "Because he is babbling that he did something that makes no sense. He said that he shot someone for three hundred dollars. His friend owes him $300." "Be in my office first thing Monday morning. I'll try to find out what's going on."

On Sunday morning, I was reading the local newspaper and on the second page was an article about a high school student who was arrested and being held in jail. He's accused of shooting his friend's father in the head and killing him. My heart stopped beating and fear raced through my body. It has to be Jimmy Dixson. I prayed to God that it wasn't, but it just had to be him. Sunday evening, I called my principal to let him know what happened and who I was pretty sure was the shooter. He agreed that it was probably Jimmy. I didn't sleep Sunday night.

Monday morning couldn't come soon enough. When I arrived at my office, Mrs. Dixson was already there. She told me that Jimmy was acting crazy. He keeps talking about killing someone. I asked her if she thought he could be involved in the shooting of her neighbor. "Oh, heavens no." We talked about what needed to take place before he would be allowed back into school. When she left, I had a sick feeling in my stomach.

Later that morning, we found out that Jimmy Dixson had been arrested for the murder of his friend's father. When the details came out, we were all in shock at what took place. Jimmy's friend promised to pay him three hundred dollars to shoot and kill his father. Jimmy drank almost a fifth of gin before going over to his neighbor's house at midnight, where he shot him in the head with a high-powered rifle while he was asleep.

I was a good friend of one of the detectives who worked on the Dixson case. He knew that I had Jimmy in my office many times. I think he wanted to know if there was any way anyone could see this coming. "At times, I had to discipline him for skipping school and he was always very, very quiet. He didn't want to talk. He never wanted to make eye contact, but when he did there wasn't any light in his eyes. They were totally dark, like Charlie Manson's."

The detective asked Jimmy if there was anyone at the school that he would want to harm. He said that he would enjoy killing one of the P.E. teachers because he was a phony S.O.B. "What about Colbo? What do you think of him?" "Even though he kicked me out of school, he's OK. He never lied to me."

The Court sentenced Jimmy to life in prison. Because he was a minor, he had to go to Miles City Reform School until he turned eighteen and then he would be sent to Montana State Prison in good old Deer Lodge. Jimmy had a tough time at Miles City. He got into several fights and tried to escape a bunch of times. From Miles City, he was sent to Warm Springs, the state mental institution for evaluation before he was sent to prison. While at Warm Springs, he hanged himself. His memory haunts me to this day. How could we have saved him? I just don't know and probably never will.

Some more terrible stuff was going on around Hellgate that most of Missoula wouldn't believe could happen in our cozy little town. I received a call from an F.B.I. agent who lived in Butte, Montana, telling me he needed to meet with me as soon as possible. He told me that there are some black guys from Las Vegas who were living in a house in North Missoula. They were finding vulnerable girls, getting them hooked on drugs and then transporting them to Vegas to become prostitutes. He said: "I have some photos I want you to look at, and some of them are hard to look at. You need to see them to see if you recognize any of the girls in the photos." I won't relate the horror I saw. I almost threw up. I didn't recognize any of the girls. That was a blessing.

I was determined to do everything in my power to help break up this ring of monsters. I suspected there must be some students who might know something about what was going on. For about three weeks, I asked a lot of students a lot of questions, but no one was talking. I wasn't getting anywhere.

Then I caught a break. I brought a junior boy into my office for chewing snoose and spitting it into the drinking fountains. He chewed four cans of Copenhagen a day. He had his lower lip removed because of the massive amount of chew he was consuming. Being really smart, he was now putting chew in his upper lip. I let him know he was qualified as the dumbest person I ever met. I also asked him if he knew anything about some black men from Las Vegas recruiting girls to become prostitutes by hooking them on drugs. "Hell, yes, they got my little sister who has been missing for over a month. I know she was doing drugs with some older dudes from out of town." "Do you know where they live?" "Yep, they live about three blocks from me." I was glad he came in, but damn, it was hard to look at him.

I called my F.B.I. friend and told him what I found out. A month went by and I hadn't heard from him. Finally, he called. "I've got some very good news for you. We busted up the Las Vegas ring and arrested eleven people who were involved." "Thank the good lord. I hope all eleven rot in hell!'"

Another disturbing thing that happened at Hellgate involved two sophomore girls. They came to Missoula from California. I always met new students to see how they were doing. They seemed to be extremely shy and would not make eye contact with me. They didn't want to visit at all. After they left, I called their counselor and asked her if she thought there was something unusual about the girls. She said, "without a doubt. When I asked them about their father, whom they live with, they would clam up. I think something is very wrong." We called the sheriff's department to see if they could dig up some information on the father. What we found out was that he wasn't their father and instead, was their stepfather. Also, he had kidnapped the girls from their mother. He had a fairly long arrest record. He got a job working at a gas station near Hellgate.

Working with the Sheriff's Department, we arranged to have the girls flown back to their mother while stepdad was at work. That should have been the end of it, but it was far from over. Somebody at the Sheriff's Department messed up big time. Stepdad found out what we did and called our little counselor and said he was coming to Hellgate to straighten her out. Stepdad was a big ugly guy who could have gotten a leading role in the movie "Deliverance." I ran down to the counselor's office to wait for this creep. He was already there. He had the counselor cornered. I grabbed his shoulder and spun him around to face me. "Keep your mouth shut and listen to me for your own good. The police are on the way here to arrest you. If you so much as blink, I'll be delighted to restrain you." Being the nutcase I was, I was hoping he would try something. I had found out he was molesting the girls. He glared at me, but didn't move. It seemed like forever until the police arrived ten minutes later. They handcuffed him and took him away. We never heard from him again. I prayed for those poor little girls.

One afternoon, I brought in a little freckled-faced sophomore boy who was frequently skipping school. Let's just call him Archie. "Archie, did you skip school yesterday?" "I sure did, and I skipped first and second period today. But I don't need to go to school no more cause I'm rich and I don't need this school stuff." "What do you mean you're rich?" "Well, I just found a bunch of money in the dumpster behind the real estate place across the street." "You did?" "Yes, sir. I already counted it and it's ten grand." "Really? Where is it?" "It's in my coat." He had to look in three or four pockets before he found an envelope with the money in it. "Have you told anyone about what you found?" "Only a couple of my buddies." "Do not tell anyone else what you found." "Why?" "Because it's probably drug money and if the dealer finds out you have his money, you are toast." "You mean, they could kill me?" "They could and probably would for ten thousand dollars." "Hold still, I'm going to call the police and ask them to come here to see you and then take possession of the money." "You mean, I don't get to keep it?" "Not necessarily, if no one shows up to claim it after a certain amount of time, then it's yours. I think it's 45 days. Then it's yours. The good news is that the drug people probably won't walk into the police station to claim it." What would they say? "Where's my drug money?" Remember, not a word to anyone if you don't want the bad guys looking for you."

I told my principal about what happened. He said, "sure as the dickens, if he gets the money, he will buy a car and drop out of school." So, we waited and after 45 days, I received a call from the police saying no one claimed the money, so it's Archie's. The next two days, no sign of Archie at school. No one answered at his home. I was standing outside with my principal, looking for any trouble, when lo and behold, none other than Archie pulled up to the curb in a very old small yellow sedan. He rolled down his window and said "Hey, Mr. C, thanks for the advice, I got my ten grand, bought this car and I'm dropping out of school." "Can we change your mind about dropping out?" "Not a chance!" He rolled up his window and off he went grinning like a Cheshire cat. I often wondered what happened to Archie.

Years after I left Hellgate, I was coming back to Missoula from a sales trip and arrived in town a little after midnight. I stopped at a convenience store to get some gas and to buy a snack for the ride home. Going inside, I was greeted by a young man who was working behind the counter. He said "Hey, Mr. Colbo, I bet you never thought I would get a really good job like this." "Being honest, I actually thought you could end up in prison. So, hey, I'm proud of you for getting this nice job." "Well, I wanted to thank you for scaring the shit out of me when I was doing drugs. You convinced me that I was going to prison if I didn't stop. I hardly did any after that." I drove home thinking, now that's a win. You never know how you may impact a person by how you interact with them. Educators may not really know until many years later. Over the years, I have received many emails, calls and letters from former students thanking me for scaring the crap out of them, causing them to stop killing themselves and ruining their lives. Saving just one of the little buggers makes it all worthwhile.

During my second summer at Hellgate, I decided it would be a good idea to have a leadership conference at Lubrecht Forest, where the University of Montana did forestry research. The facility had twelve cabins and a nice conference center. I was a friend of Hank, who ran the place, so I asked him if it would be possible to hold our conference there. No hesitation, he said yes. He thought it was a great idea.

I know what you're thinking… you're thinking that all of the student council members and some honor society members would be invited to attend. Nope! At Hellgate, we had several groups of students that had their leaders. For example, the dirtheads were a group of tough kids mainly from the North side of Missoula, which was the poorest part of town. They hung out during the noon hour across the street in back of Hellgate. They were there to raise whatever hell they could think of, just short of being arrested.

The second group, I called the zombies. They dressed in all black and looked like they were starving to death. They seldom spoke above a whisper, never made eye contact and were more than a little spooky.

The next group were kids who weren't great students nor were they athletes. They never got into trouble, attended school unless they were sick and went on to graduate and I had little or no idea who most of them were. They never got any special recognition or awards. They were just good kids that we should have paid more attention to.

Of course, another group was the jocks who certainly had their leaders. The last group was the nerds. They were very smart, but seemed to lack social skills. They sort of stuck to themselves and had a tough time relating to the rest of the student body.

Out of these groups and a couple more, I put together a list of 24 students. Next, I had to talk eight teachers into giving up three days of their summer vacation to be chaperones and speakers at the conference. I picked the best of the best to come to the camp, teachers who could relate to all students without regard for anything other than they loved younger people and saw the potential for success in every student. An example was one of our industrial arts teachers, Dan "The Man" Gilman. Dan is one of the most unique men I have ever met. In my opinion, he not only was a great industrial arts instructor, but was the best track coach I ever observed, and no one else is even close. He coached the Knights, and his shot-putters set many records and at one time, he had several of his throwers chucking the shot over 60 feet. Unheard of! His discus thrower still holds the state record. If I had a student who was about to drop out of school or was causing problems, I sent them to Dan. Not once did I have any discipline problem with them again. And talk about a character! One example was, Dan called our principal "Merit Man" because he smoked Merit cigarettes. For twelve years, Dan found articles in newspapers and magazines that were about the risk of smoking. Every morning, he put an article on Dick Correll's desk. Dick, being somewhat of a character himself, kept all the articles and on the last day he was Hellgate's Principal, he called a teachers' meeting to say goodbye. Dan was in the front row of the meeting. Dick walked over to him with this huge box and lifted the box up and dumped all twelve years of articles on Dan's head. Who says teachers' meetings have to be boring? More on that subject later.

Back to the conference. After getting settled in and getting cabin assignments done, we had the kids explore a little and then we had a barbeque, making sure the kids stuffed themselves with hamburgers and hot dogs. Next, we all met in the conference room to explain why they were chosen to be here. Also, I wanted them to know why each teacher was chosen. Next, I wanted them to understand the rooming assignments. For example, a zombie was rooming with a jock. You talk about a stretch. Of course, some of them looked at me like I must have lost my mind. Lastly, I told them we would get all of them up at 7 A.M. for a walk or a run. For some of them, I had just removed all doubt about my being nuts. I was pretty sure the zombies had never walked fast, let alone run, unless maybe they were being chased by the police. This should be good.

I could hardly wait for 7:00 to roll around. At 5 before 7, we started knocking on cabin doors, waking some of them up. They were surprised, somewhat shocked and most were dismayed. They thought I was kidding. We told them they didn't have to run, but at least had to walk. The zombies walked very, very slowly. I guess they were making sure they wouldn't sweat, causing their mascara to run and ruin their look. Some ran, some walked, some hardly moved – it was a great start.

After breakfast, the conference began in earnest. We started by having all of the students stand up and introduce themselves and then tell us one thing that bothered them the most about going to high school at Hellgate. I emphasized that there were no incorrect answers. Even our little zombies quietly took part. I was a little surprised, but very pleased.

Next, I introduced all of the teachers I picked to speak at the conference. It was important that the student leaders know why these teachers were chosen. Another example was Byron Anderson, a 6'4" and 240-pound science teacher who was a highly decorated marine who saw a lot of combat in Vietnam. Andy never talked about his war experience. The kids had no idea he was a wounded hero. I proceeded to let the students know how special every teacher in attendance was.

Throughout the day, each teacher gave their presentations and there was lots of valuable interaction with the student leaders. The day ended after I talked about my fifty-pound little hero, David Farber, who I dedicated a chapter to in this book. Without question, learning about David had a positive impact on the leaders.

During the second evening, we kept the kids entertained with lots of games and a ton of 'smores. The local dentists would be pleased with the number of cavities we created. What I hoped for was happening. All of the leaders were meeting and socializing with all of the other leaders. There were no cliques. It did my heart good to see a zombie talking with and enjoying the company of a jock. My crazy plan was working!

The next morning after breakfast, we wrapped up the conference with each student telling us what they gained by being at the conference. I was proud of how sincere they were. They clearly understood that they had way more in common with each other than differences. At the core, they pretty much had the same needs and fears. I had a big smile on my face all the way back to Missoula.

After school started, I was supervising the lunchroom during the noon hour when I saw something that made my day. Matt Bitney, another hero of mine, has been in a wheelchair his entire life. He has never been able to walk. It was difficult for Matt to get through the food line. The leader of the dirtheads, Bret Rodgers, who never, ever ate lunch in the cafeteria, was helping Matt get his lunch and then wheeled him over to a table. Bret sat next to Matt and visited with him while they ate their lunches. Bret, the former so-called dirthead, now has a nice business carving bears and other animals out of wood with a chainsaw. He's a very talented artist. Watching Matt and Bret eating lunch together made the time and effort of putting on the leadership conference totally worth it.

CHAPTER 15

Dick Hits His Stride

In 1981, we had a teacher strike at Missoula County Schools. It escalated into a really nasty affair. Being an Assistant Principal is not a pleasant place to be when a strike happens. You are stuck in the middle. You need to keep the support of the teachers, and somehow you also have to carry out the orders of the Administration. My lousy assignment was to lead the substitute teachers (scabs) across the picket lines. Twice, I led them across the line without anyone helping me. When I got off the bus to lead the subs in, I warned the striking teachers not to touch me and not to spit on me. I watched teachers change from being mild-mannered, polite and respectful human beings, to boisterous, obnoxious, vulgar and angry people. I now understand the power of the mob. I was hurt and saddened seeing nice folks turn into thugs.

After the fifth day of the strike, it was clear that both parties were dug in. The administration knew that the teachers were planning on stopping the subs from going into the schools again at all costs. They were planning on having parents and students join them on the picket line.

An emergency meeting was called for all administrators in the district to meet at the administration building on Wednesday evening. A discussion was to take place on the best way to break the strike. Our Superintendent was a burly older gentleman who played football for Oregon State when they played in the Rose Bowl. He talked about the strike using military terminology. He said, "the Assistant Principals were working in the trenches. We must penetrate the line on Friday with as much force as possible. This could lead us to ultimate victory." What???

I just couldn't take any more of the "we" stuff. I knew full-well what I was going to say would kill any chance of advancement up the administrative ladder, but what he wanted to do was just flat out wrong, and someone was going to get hurt.

Oh well, so much for advancement. I said: "What's this *we* stuff, George? I haven't seen you around when I took the subs across the line and into the school. The teachers are angry, and with parents and students on the picket line, someone, and perhaps all of the people are going to be injured badly. If you insist on breaking the line at Hellgate, I'll do it on one condition and that is if you show up and lead the teachers in with me." George's face turned red while I was talking. If looks could kill, I was dead. After what seemed an eternity, Dick C, my Principal at the time, said: "Ken's right and we definitely should **not** try to cross the line on Friday." Our red-faced Superintendent said: "Does anyone else think like they do?" Several hands went up. "School will be closed until further notice."

On the following Tuesday, the strike ended, with no one getting hurt or mentally screwed up for the rest of their lives. A school board member's horse was shot and killed but no one ever found out who did it. Who knows who the creep was? It took years for hard feelings to go away. Some never did. There are no winners in a strike.

In the district, it was common knowledge that if our Superintendent wanted you fired or moved out of the district, he would invite you to lunch at Don's Restaurant. Some of my goofball teacher and counselor friends set up a pool at Hellgate. The winner would come closest to guessing when George would ask Ken to have lunch with him. In a week and two days, in came the call to my secretary. George wanted to buy me lunch.

I gathered up a couple of documents and went to Don's to meet with the commander-in-chief. There he sat, looking very regal and more than ready to convince me that he had a great opportunity for me out of his district. I told George I wasn't going to sit down. "Why not?" "Because I'm not going to move out of the district. In fact, I'm not going anywhere except back to Hellgate! I brought my performance evaluation where you stated that I was the best assistant principal you have ever seen in your entire career. So, you can't fire me. I was right about not crossing the line and besides, I saved you some money because I'm not eating lunch. Have a nice day!"

I hesitated writing anything about the strike, but I thought it was important to point out how awful a strike can be. I'll always believe I did the right thing when I stood up to George. He retired two years after the strike, and I was still at Hellgate. George was actually a nice man and an effective Superintendent.

While at Hellgate, I started jogging after work, more than anything to maintain some sanity. I'm not built for running. I'm built much better for lifting heavy things. My principal, Dick, who stood up for me in the strike, was really into running and was a good athlete. He was a very stylish runner. I told Dick I might run in a ten-mile race, which started in Bonner, Montana, and finished in downtown Missoula. Dickster said "I don't suppose you want to make a little wager on the race?" "Hey, sure, why not?" "How about twenty smackers?"

The race was two months away and I jogged six times a week and was getting into pretty fair shape. About two weeks before race day, Dick asked me if I wanted to go on a little run with him. He was checking me out. I met Tricky Dickey at his house, and we agreed to run up the Rattlesnake, a beautiful area that enters a wilderness forest. When I arrived at his house, he was prancing around supposedly warming up. He looked damn snazzy in his expensive running shoes and jogging outfit.

Off we went. I sort of knew where we were going, but I fell in behind Dickster. Hey, I know about drafting. Cripes, I was running faster than I was used to, and I couldn't keep up. At the turnaround point, Dickster was doing pushups. He looked at me and asked if I got lost. I told him I was busy checking out the terrain. He knew I was fibbing.

Well, hell, he took off for his house and beat me back to his place by at least a half mile. I had zero chance of beating him. I thought about faking an injury for just a minute. No! I had to show up. After a lot of thought, I came up with a plan.

I asked four of my teacher buddies, who were going to watch the race, if they would mind locating themselves at four different places along the race. I told them to stand close to the runners so when Dick comes by, he could see them. When he would ask, as he undoubtedly would, if they've seen Ken, tell him no. He will think I'm behind him. One of the teachers stood on a bridge that Tricky Dick had to run under. I guess Dick looked up and was told "No, Ken hasn't been here yet!"

I arrived at where the start of the race was and saw Dick near the front of the runners and his head was on a swivel. He wanted to find me. I spotted a friend of mine, who is 6'6" and a wide body. I quickly told him what was going on and that I was going to hide behind him.

When the starting gun went off, I ran as fast as I could to a barrow pit on the side of the road. Running down the barrow pit, I could go ahead of Dick and he wouldn't see me. Once I was sure I was ahead of my boss, I ran onto the road.

I ran at about 80% of what I normally would do, cruising along and having a good time. As I passed each teacher, I reminded them to tell Dick that they hadn't seen me. At the end of the race, you had to circle around a little park to the finish line. Once I got to about four hundred yards of the finish line, I ran as fast as I could. I almost puked. I spotted Dick's wife waiting for him by the finish line. I said hello to her. She looked like she saw a ghost. She said, "I didn't think you had a chance of beating him." "I actually can't, I just tricked him."

I saw Dick running around the park in his stylish manner, cruising toward the finish line. He had a huge smile on his face. He was so darn happy. Then, I stepped out of the crowd and went to the finish line. When Dick was about thirty yards from the finish, I leaned out and waved at him. He acted like somebody shot him. He had a bewildered look on his kisser. He managed to say, "How the hell, what in the world happened, you're not supposed to be here!" I told him, "Sometimes you just can't trust some of the teachers at Hellgate." "I'm not going to talk to you for a month!" "Not even a word?" "Nope." "Well, you already said one word." For a month, he never said a word to me. He communicated by sending me notes. As he was always one of my best friends, I apologized for being such a devious rascal.

"If it will make you feel better, I promise next year, I will line up next to you and we will do double or nothing." "Now, that's more like it."

The next year, Dick was hurt and couldn't run. I ran seven-minute miles for my best time ever. I averaged running ten miles a day. One day, I ran thirty miles. Sure as could be, I was punishing myself for being such a sneaker (not the kind you wear running.)

CHAPTER 16

Fun and Games in the Big Hole

Because I was just a bouncer with a Master's Degree at Hellgate, I needed to find ways to stop thinking about Hellgate all the time. Sentinel Principal, Dick Correll, my Principal at Hellgate, Don Harbaugh, and Hellgate Wrestling Coach Lanny Bryant and I decided to go fishing in the Big Hole Valley in Southwestern Montana. Lanny knew how to catch some lunkers out of the Horse Prairie Creek. We flipped a coin and Dick became our designated driver. The rest of us passengers drank a few beers on the way over. Our destination was Dillon, where we planned to stay overnight before heading out for Horse Prairie Creek.

Don Harbaugh, of course we called him Hardbrow, was raised on a ranch near Jordan, Montana. His folks' ranch was next to Benny Binion's ranch, the same Binion who owned the Horseshoe Casino in Las Vegas. Rumor had it that you could buy a machine gun from the Binions. I'm not sure, I never saw a need for having a machine gun.

Anyway, Don said, after a few beers, "even a weak cowboy can take down any wrestler. We were raised branding cattle which is no easy chore, and you had to be darn tough to get the job done!" Our 5'6", 150- pound Lanny said, "no way you can take me off my feet." Old 6'2", 200-pound Don, being certain of his prowess, countered with "you are nowhere as strong as the critters we branded, and they were really unhappy to have their butts burned!"

I saw an opportunity to have some real fun. I suggested that when we get to Dillon, we should find a park and see who could take down who. Or is it whom? Not sure.

By the time we found a suitable park in Dillon, both combatants had consumed several more beers. Both were now in top-notch condition. I volunteered to coach Hardbrow because of my wrestling background. Of course, I was going to give him really bad advice. They were to start facing each other and, on my command, charge each other to see who would take the other one down. Don went in hard, following my advice and Lanny had him airborne, then slammed him into the turf using what is called a fireman's carry. Lanny used this move many times on his way to becoming an all-American wrestler. Don had no clue. I told him he just didn't go in fast enough and not near high enough. Just the opposite of what he should do. Hee-hee. Undaunted, our cowboy charged time and time again, with absolutely no success. I think Don made about twenty attempts. My count could have been a little off. Don sure could take a beating. He could bounce off the hard ground an unbelievable number of times.

A rather large crowd of Dilloners began to gather around to watch our knot-heads. They thought they were fighting for real. I tried to explain to them that they were just having a friendly game of Slam the Cowboy into the turf. Cowboy Don finally couldn't stand up. He grudgingly conceded. Being his friends, we carried him over to the car. He was alive, but looked like warmed over death.

We heard that, by far, the cheapest hotel in Dillon was located by the railroad tracks on the north side of town. It was called the Metland. I swear I didn't know how the Metland was still standing. It seemed to be leaning over, ready to fall down with the slightest breeze. It hadn't been painted in decades. The railroad track went by only a few feet from the worn-out building. The good news, we heard music coming out of the Metland, there was a dance going on. Yahoo!! As soon as we got inside, it looked like the dance was for senior citizens only. Most seemed like it might be the last dance they would ever have. The dancers were, just guessing, between 90 and deceased. We weren't about to let a few wrinkles and saggy skin deter us from dancing with those neat old chicks. Younger chickens probably wouldn't want to dance with us anyway. They sure appreciated our willingness to jitterbug. We danced until they closed the joint. Our cowboy wrestler just sat there, watching.

We knew we had chosen the right place to bunk because we scored a room for $24 and it included two beds and two roll-aways. We couldn't beat that with a stick. There were a few minor drawbacks, however. We asked the bartender to give us a wake-up call at 6:00 am. He politely said, "damn rights." Once inside the room, I knew this was going to be a long four hours until our wake-up call. I laid down on my roll-away and it collapsed so much that my toes were only about a foot away from my nose and I'm really inflexible.

I finally dozed off and then I swore the train was coming through our room. It missed us but left a lot of dust floating around the room.

Sometime, stand about ten feet from a speeding train as it goes by, and you'll get the picture. I do give some credit to the Metland because we did get our wake-up call. It went something like this: "Wake up you sons of bitches, it's six!" This very pleasant notice was given by the janitor who also cleaned up the joint. His two roles were to clean the place and to scare the bejeesus out of the guests with his wake-up calls.

After breakfast, we drove to Horse Prairie Creek. I had fished Horse Prairie with Lanny and we caught some lunkers in the slow-moving deep stream. I hurried over to my favorite spot, and on the third cast, landed a nice two-pound rainbow trout. Not bad, if I do say so myself. Fishing was really good, and after about two hours, I met up with Dick and Lanny and asked them if they had seen our Cowboy Wrestler anywhere. They hadn't seen him. I saw a little knoll about two hundred yards away so I walked over to it to see if I could spot Don. Holy Crap! What I saw scared me! I saw Don spread-eagled on the ground in the middle of a bunch of sagebrush. I thought he was dead. I got to him as fast as I could run. Thank the good Lord, he opened his eyes and mumbled something about he was so sore that even his hair hurt. It took about twenty minutes to convince him that he could stand up. Stand up he did, in sections. He covered the three hundred yards to the car in the slowest time possible without walking backwards.

Off we went to stay in Lanny's cabin at the Elkhorn resort that was located next to the thriving metropolis of Polaris, population 31, give or take a couple that may or may not live there full-time.

It was almost mandatory that we stop to have a beer at the Polaris bar. The owner of the bar was Walt Metcalf. He was also the postmaster, ski lift operator, unofficial mayor and worm-digger if you needed any for fishing. The Polaris bar had two tables and six stools, that's it. There was only one customer at the bar, an old ranch hand who was very weathered and grizzled. He no doubt came out of the hay fields in the Big Hole Valley. I bet Don, whose hair still hurt, that he couldn't get the old timer to say anything but "yep" and "nope" in the first five questions he asked him. I lost because he said "maybe" on the fourth question he was asked. Heading back to Missoula, we were all in agreement that we had a damn good weekend.

Oh, and just in case the readers are thinking about finding their way to Horse Prairie to catch some of those lunkers, just remember this. There are grizzly bears, black bears, wolves, coyotes, snakes and man-eating gophers lurking around in the woods near the stream. Even worse, the wake-up call guy from the Metland frequently goes fishing at Horse Prairie Creek. That will keep you away if nothing else does.

CHAPTER 17

I Could Have Been a Millionaire...

I took a year's leave of absence from Hellgate to see if I could find another career other than disciplining the rascals at Hellgate High School. Automatic pinsetters eliminated my chances of being a forty-plus-year-old pinsetter with a master's plus three. I had already eliminated being a priest. For a brief moment, I considered selling used cars, but I finally decided selling insurance would be easier. What I really wanted to sell was tax-sheltered-annuities for educators. They were tax-deductible and you could put a lot of money into them. Just getting educators to save for their retirement was a good thing. How hard could it be? All I had to do was call educators whom I already knew and ask them if I could have twenty minutes of their time to see if I could make their retirement better financially. Simple, and it worked ninety percent of the time or more. My first year, I made more income selling TSAs than I did as a school administrator. Not only that, it was fun!

Because I had two daughters in undergraduate college and one working on her law degree, I felt I had to go back to Hellgate for another year. I would sell TSA's in the evening and on weekends. It was a big mistake. I hated every second of it. What you soon realize when you leave the school environment is that folks in the insurance business are much more positive and happy with their jobs than teachers are. Most teachers are very negative, and for the most part, feel like they're underpaid and not respected enough. It's been proven that comments made by teachers in faculty break rooms are 90% negative. We administrators at Hellgate tried to change that. If any teachers at Hellgate asked us how we were doing, our response always was: "We have never had it any better." I'm sure it drove the "woe is me" crowd absolutely nuts. Insurance agents had to be positive in their relationships with their clients or they wouldn't last. When you're working inside a school, you don't realize how seldom teachers laugh, and that's sad.

I began what turned out to be a thirty-four-year career in investment sales. My first office was in a basement, renting from a Kentucky Central regional agent. I didn't want to sell insurance, just TSAs. The Kentucky Central agent was bound and determined to recruit me to sell insurance. After a year, I gave in and became a licensed agent with Kentucky Central. Little did I know what I was getting myself into.

Kentucky Central was an A+ rated company located in Lexington, Kentucky. I went to Lexington to check them out. What a beautiful city. There are no slums in Lexington. The University of Kentucky is there as well as IBM's headquarters. It's surrounded by horse farms that raise and groom thoroughbred racehorses. Think Secretariat. Kentucky Central's home office was next door to Rupp Arena, home of the University of Kentucky's Wildcats. The products were excellent and the home office staff was impressive. I knew I could sell a lot of their insurance products and I did.

In my fifth year with Kentucky Central, things were about to change in a big way. An agent in Billings told me that Kentucky Central was in financial trouble. Being concerned, I called the Kentucky State Insurance Department to see if I could find out what Kentucky Central's new financial rating was going to be. Their rating was going to be B+, an alarming drop from A+. I immediately called the regional agent and he said: "It's not going to drop." "What?!?"

A week later I went to Coeur d'Alene, Idaho, to attend Kentucky Central's regional meeting. I intentionally sat in back. I waited until the Regional Agent told the audience that Kentucky Central's rating was going to remain A+. I stood and said: "That's not the truth. I talked to the Kentucky Insurance Commissioner, and he told me the rating was going to be B+." "You don't have to ask me to leave, because I'm out of here."

Worried, I looked at the insurance contracts and I discovered that I could lower my client's insurance amount to a minimum and keep them in force. Then, they could purchase a new policy with the remaining cash value and have a minimal amount of financial harm done to them. I began meeting with all of my Kentucky Central clients as fast as I could. All was going well until one evening when an English teacher friend of mine called and said: "I received a letter that I don't think you mailed. Your English isn't perfect, but it's a lot better than the grammar used in this letter. Let's meet at Hellgate tomorrow and I'll give you the letter."

I hardly slept that night wondering what the hell was going on. After I read the letter, I knew damn well what was going on. Somebody wanted me out of the insurance business. The letter essentially said that I was taking advantage of my clients to make a ton of money and earn a trip to a Hawaiian resort. I was supposed to have sent the letter to a Kentucky Central agent in Billings, thanking him for showing me how to screw my clients. My name was forged on the letter. I was going to include the letter in this book, but I never want to see it again.

I mailed all of my clients a letter letting them know about the letter they received and the forgery. I told them I wouldn't rest until I found out who was trying to destroy my career. So, who would do this? I made a list of suspects starting with the Regional General Agent and the local General Agent, as they were getting over-writes. I confronted all of the agents in the Missoula office. No one was talking. Two months went by and then I got a call from a Kentucky Central agent in Spokane. He said: "I'm mad at the Regional Agent in Missoula because the bastard took all of my clients away from me and put them in his agency." Legally, he could do this, but it's a real slimy thing to do. He said: "He forged your name. I know because I saw him do it in my office." "If this goes to court, will you stand up and say what happened?" "I damn sure will."

I had a good relationship with a well-respected attorney, so I explained to him what happened. He said: "You have a good case, but I'm booked." However, I have a new associate who would no doubt take it." I set-up a meeting with the new guy. When I first saw him, I thought he couldn't be more than fifteen years old. What I would soon discover was that he had a chip on his shoulder and was a little pit bull and he was really smart. "I want this case; it looks like a slam dunk. I'll make them pay for trying to ruin your career."

The case took over two years to complete. At one deposition, my lawyer faced nine lawyers representing Kentucky Central, the forger and a Kentucky Central Liability Company. When we sat down, my pit bull said very loudly: "It doesn't matter if there are 100 lawyers on their side, it won't matter because he's guilty."

The forger's attorneys were really quite creative. At first, they said: "there were no damages because I was already a mess." "The terrible job I had at Hellgate just about did me in." "Also, he almost went bankrupt in Lewistown running a failed sporting goods store." "His wife left him with three little daughters, and he tried to do three jobs, which resulted in his being severely depressed." "So, he's so damaged, what our client did couldn't hurt him." After using that strategy for about a month, they somehow decided that it wasn't working for them. They did a 180. Their new argument was: "We interviewed several of Ken's clients and teachers he worked with and we found out that Ken is highly respected and is considered to be a very good person and is doing very well." The next time, we met with the forger's attorneys, I couldn't help asking them which Ken Colbo I was today – the messed up one or the "I'm-doing-just-fine guy?" For over two years, my life was put on hold. The legal process is demeaning and demoralizing. I wasn't about to cave in. I'll wrap this up because just writing about it makes me sad. Of course, I won the lawsuit. The money I was awarded wasn't as important as sending a message to the forger and Kentucky Central that what they did was evil.

Soon after the lawsuit was over, it was discovered that the President of Kentucky Central was involved in a massive amount of fraud. He used Kentucky Central's funds to give loans to his own son and even to a Governor of Kentucky, and they were interest-free. This, and mismanagement, led to the total collapse of Kentucky Central. The President who was a vibrant, healthy 65-year-old, died of a massive heart attack soon after Kentucky Central's demise. In this case, crime didn't pay. One of my favorite sayings is, "Time wounds all heels." The forger left Montana, thank the Good Lord. I'm not a good enough man to forgive him, but I'm working on it.

I enjoyed selling TSA's and insurance. Because I had many friends all over the state, I did a ton of windshield time. I could go anywhere to make a sale. In the middle of January, an insurance client of mine said: "I have a referral for you. She's a cousin of mine and lives just north of Noxon, Montana. She really needs insurance." She gave me her name and number. I called her. "Sure, come on up. Do you have a good car?" "Yes." "That's good, because the snow gets pretty deep where we live." "I'm a Montanan and I can handle snow. No worries." She gave me directions. "I'll be there at 4 tomorrow."

The next day, when I left Missoula, the weather was pretty good, so off I went to Noxon. Noxon is a small community of about 400 residents. It's located about 230 miles north of Missoula. When I arrived at Noxon, there was about three feet of snow on the ground. My referral lived about seven miles north of Noxon. The first five miles, I was driving on a paved road, but then the pavement ended. My Buick LaSabre didn't have a problem pushing snow on the pavement. Off the pavement, I could barely make out the car tracks in the snow that were leading to my destination. I was pushing snow that was now above my bumper. I was told to just keep following the tracks until you see a house. I got high centered about three hundred yards from their home. Walking to their house, the snow was above my knees. Their home was a small cabin. I knocked on the door and a frail, scraggly-looking woman stepped out to greet me. "You must be Ken?" "Yes, ma'am." She said: "I need to tell you not to look at Fred, my husband, because he hates insurance salesmen. Please, please don't look at him." "OK, I won't look at Fred, no problem."

Entering the dimly lit cabin, I couldn't help myself – I had to quickly glance at Fred. I thought I had arrived in the Ozarks and the movie Deliverance popped into my demented mind. Herman Munster also found his way into my thinking. Fred was a huge, hairy, toothless guy. I didn't look at him again, as I didn't want to die in a cabin north of Noxon.

We sat down at the kitchen table next to a wood burning stove. I got down to business and asked Mrs. Herman what kind of insurance she was interested in. "That term stuff. The cheapest you've got." "Well, the longer the term, the more expensive it is." "Then give me short term." "I need to ask if you are in good health." "Boy, am I ever. Oh, I had a little problem about six weeks ago when I was out drinking and dancing with Fred over there in the corner. When, bam, and down I went. I had one of those things that go off in your head." "Do you mean you had an aneurysm?" "Yea, that's it, but I'm OK now." "Well, I'm sorry but you probably will be declined for any life insurance." "Are you sure?" "Pretty darn sure." "Hey Ken, if I behave myself, maybe you could come back in the summer and then I could get some of that term stuff." "Maybe … I'd better go now." I glanced at Fred again before leaving. I thought I saw him look over at the rifle hanging on the wall.

I managed to get the car turned around and headed back to Missoula. About 50 miles from Noxon, there is a 30-mile straight stretch of highway. There was little or no traffic, so I stomped on the gas pedal. I went about five miles and was sailing along going 90 miles an hour when a highway patrolman put on his flashing lights as I went by. Scared the bejesus out of me. He pulled me over. Why would he do that, other than I was going at about thirty miles an hour over the speed limit. He told me that about a week ago, somebody ran into a moose at night on this same stretch of road and rolled his car. "He didn't survive, and I don't want you to be another death on this highway. I'm going to fine you $80.00." It was a long ride home. I vowed to be a lot more careful about referrals. I figured I lost about $200 on the day, but at least Fred didn't shoot me.

I had an interesting opportunity to make a huge insurance sale in my second year as an insurance agent. My commission on the sale would have allowed me to retire comfortably. Here's what happened. I want you to know that for my own well-being, I'm leaving out names of the major participants.

A friend of mine in Missoula told me that a relative of his was interested in buying some insurance for his charitable organization. He was a minister in Los Angeles. I gave him a call. He gave me some specifics, which I got really excited about. Apparently, there were 8 board members sitting as advisors on his organization. They were all in their late sixties or older. He said they wanted to do a very sophisticated insurance policy which would benefit each member monetarily and also protect the interests of his non-profit charity. It was called reverse split-dollar. I'll spare you the details. Each member was to receive a policy with a $5,000,000 death benefit. My commission would have been a little north of $800,000. I knew I needed help with the illustrations and presentation of the product. I called Kentucky Central and asked for this help. Wow! Not only would they help with the illustrations, but they would fly one of their vice presidents out to L.A. to make the presentation to the Board. I spent the better part of a week making sure I knew the details of reverse split dollar backwards, forwards and upside down. The following week, off I went to meet the minister and his board members.

When the Kentucky Central Vice President and I arrived in the parking lot, I couldn't help but notice that the cars in the parking lot were Mercedes, Cadillacs, a Jaguar and a couple of other extremely expensive vehicles. Hey, this has to be the real deal! We were led into a conference room where introductions were made. After introductions, the minister asked me to come into his office. He asked me to please sign a couple documents as a witness. I said: "I need to read them before I sign them." "We're in a hurry, please just sign them and then we can go back and get the meeting started." I didn't want to upset him, but I wasn't about to sign anything without knowing what I was signing. So, I didn't sign. The minister was angry, but nevertheless led me back into the conference room where everyone involved was waiting for our entrance.

What an impressive group of distinguished gentlemen were waiting for my presentation about reverse split dollar insurance. I did notice that one of their accountants was sweating profusely, even though the room was air conditioned. "Before I explain and review the illustrations we have for you, I will need to see your corporate documents." The minister said: "There is absolutely no need for that." "Yes, there is." I like to use the phrase "Let me see if I've got this right", when I know something stinks to high heaven. So, I said, "Let me see if I've got this right. You want me to sign documents without reading them, don't want me to see your corporate documents, and you, being the obviously very bright and accomplished businessmen that you are, decided that you want a second-year insurance agent from Montana to write the applications for what would probably be the largest sale ever made by a Kentucky Central insurance agent? You chose the wrong person. I'm insulted that you think I'm that naïve and stupid. I'm leaving now and don't even think about stopping me." The Vice President grabbed my arm to try to stop me from leaving. I told him to keep his hands off me and that he could stay if he wanted to. He did and that didn't surprise me. Later, I found out he was up to his ears in the fraud that brought on the demise of Kentucky Central.

I flew home thinking maybe I could be wrong, but my gut told me I was right, and I was. The "do-gooders" were indeed laundering money. It was later disclosed that the German Mafia was behind the scam. The sweating accountant left the country, never to be heard from again. Greed is an unbelievable evil force. Why in the world all of these successful businessmen would involve themselves in this kind of crime is beyond me. I'll never understand any of it. Over my thirty plus years in the investment industry, I was made aware of several pyramid schemes. I always wondered why the instigator spent so much time and energy involving themselves in criminal activities when they could have put that effort into doing legal business and becoming very successful.

About in the middle of my investment career, I received a call from my nephew who was living in Deer Lodge, working as a physical therapist. He told me he visited a very elderly lady who was a cousin of his. She lived alone on her ranch near Garrison, Montana. He said he noticed that she had some suspicious documents on her kitchen table. She said that two Elders from the Jehovah Witness Church asked her to sign them because they wanted to look out for her best financial interests. At the time, this dear old lady was ninety-six years old. She had spent her entire adult life living on the ranch. Her husband had died several years before. She had never had a driver's license. Other than my nephew, who was a distant cousin, there were no relatives anywhere close to her. She was truly alone. Thank goodness my nephew checked on her once in a while.

I told my nephew to call the State Auditor's office if you're reasonably sure that a possible fraud is taking place. He called them a short time later. Finding that there were enough questionable documents and inappropriate life insurance policies in existence, the Auditor's office became involved in the case. About a week went by when I received a call from a Missoula attorney whom I know, who asked me if I would be willing to look at all of the insurance policies and then try to recoup the cash value and premiums. I told him I was more than happy to become involved in getting some of Una's money back.

What happened was, her two so-called advisor friends had sold her ranch without her knowledge. They sold it for over six million dollars. They told her she had to move into Deer Lodge because it wasn't safe for her to stay at the ranch. She had to be moved because the new owners of the ranch would soon be showing up. Her benevolent advisors purchased her a dumpy little house in a poor neighborhood in Deer Lodge for approximately thirty thousand dollars. How generous of these crooks.

The insurance policies I looked at were all basically the same. Going forward, I'll start using the thief's names, which I think are Willis and Ericson. They designed the policies in the following manner. They invested the maximum amount of cash they could put into them based on the amount of insurance they applied for. The idea is to hold the maximum funded policies for a few years, then lower the amount of insurance to a minimum required amount, usually twenty-five thousand, leaving enough cash in them so they wouldn't lapse. Then, they were going to take out zero-cost loans, borrowing out all of the cash value without paying any taxes on the cash value when the death benefits were issued.

It took very little time for me to discover who the agent was that was making huge commissions writing the applications for these policies. He lived in North Dakota. His phone number was all over the applications, so I could hardly wait to call him. After he answered, I remember telling him that I knew exactly what he had done and that the State of Montana Auditor's office also knew what he did. I said to him: "You will begin calling all of the life insurance companies that issued these fraudulent policies and get all of the premiums invested in them and all the cash that's in them." "You will being calling as soon as I am done talking." "If you do what is in your best interests and get all of the funds back to the Estate of Una Iverson, perhaps you will spend less time in prison." I gave him the address of the law firm that he should request the funds be sent. All he said was: "I understand." I didn't know if he could be sent to prison for his involvement, but it sounded good. My intent was to scare the crap out of him. Apparently, I got the job done. Approximately $800,000 was sent back to Una's Estate from the policies.

Five attorneys, all working on Una's behalf, and two accountants were called to meet at one of the attorney's conference rooms at his office. I was invited to attend. Their mistake. After some chit chat, the lead attorney got down to business. He said, "the purpose of the meeting is to get an update on the progress being made to recover assets for Una's estate." "Ken, why don't you go first." "Gladly – I'm happy to tell you that a little over $800,000 has been recovered for Una out of the bogus life insurance policies." There were several nods of appreciation and a couple of "that a boy's." "My part in this endeavor seems to be done. But, before I leave, I have a couple of questions for you. Why are there five attorneys meeting here today? It seems to me that one good attorney could get the job done. I know that you all are corresponding among yourselves and charging Una's Estate for all of this duplication." I shocked the lawyers into silence. That's hard to do, by the way. "Also, why two accountants, when one good accountant could get the job done?" "I know you're upset with me, I don't' care. I have gotten back over $800,000 and am not being compensated one penny, which is what I want. How much have you recovered, net of your fees? All I am trying to do is look out for Una. She's been damaged enough. I suppose Pro Bono is out of the question. I know you all are going to be very pleased that I'm leaving now." Out I went, knowing I probably didn't make an impact on how they billed, but I had to let them know how I felt. It's been hard for me to get the assistant principal in charge of discipline out of my character.

This turned out to be the largest financial fraud case in the history of Montana. Somewhere around six and one-half million, Willis and Erickson had set up an elaborate complicated system of trusts and interlocking companies to hide their evil doings. They lived in expensive houses, had very expensive cars, traveled abroad and by and large, had a really nice time spending Una's money. It was also discovered that Willis made a $400,000 brokerage fee for selling Una's ranch. They even spent 2 million, trying to set up a foreign capital depository where the super-rich could have a place to hide their money, similar to using offshore banks. So, they had enough brain power to construct these complicated scams, but obviously were two greedy bastards who just were not satisfied with earning an honest living.

During the trial, Willis pleaded for mercy from the Court because he was so ill that he thought he only had a year or two to live. Sometimes, really smart people can do incredibly dumb things. The judge in the case informed Willis that jails and prisons all have surveillance cameras. A tape was played showing the sickly Willis jogging and lifting weights. Nice try, Willis!

I made a point of seeing Una at her little house in Deer Lodge. I found her to be an amazing woman. She was one of the most positive ladies I've ever met. She lived to be 106 years old. I asked her what was the secret to her longevity. She said: "I think the most helpful thing is that every day, while I'm having breakfast, I think, what will I do today that is new to me." "It might be that I'll walk to a new place, or I might visit with someone that I've never talked to." The last time I saw Una, she was 101 and she looked like she could be in her seventies. She actually felt sorry for Willis and Erickson because she said, "they were so young, and they ruined the rest of their lives." It's a shame more people didn't have the pleasure of meeting Una. Finally, Willis and Erickson were sentenced to fifteen years in good old Montana State Prison. I hope they both found some nice big old boyfriends.

Chapter 18

It Just Wasn't My Time

There have been many times in my life that I came very, very close to dying. Here are some of my brushes with death:

I had a long, seven-hour hip-replacement surgery that required removing eight cables that were holding my old replacement together. I was resting in my hospital bed, talking to my wife who came to see if I was doing OK. I was watching the Weather Channel and I said, 'I need to get all of my clients out of the stock market, look at what it is doing'. I babbled a little more nonsense. Knowing I was in big trouble, my wife ran out of the room to get a nurse. The next thing I knew, I was in a warm room, looking at a fellow who I didn't know. 'Where am I?' You're in Intensive Care, and you're going to live. 'Your oxygen level dropped to 30% of normal, because you had a blood clot. Luckily, you didn't die and probably won't have any brain damage'. He didn't know how much my poor brain had already been damaged.

Hospitals make more money if they can get you out of there ASAP. I knew I wasn't up to getting out of bed and walking around. I should have said, 'No'. They got me out of bed, I went about 30 yards, grabbed a waste-paper basket, and threw up into it. The embarrassing part is when I bent over, I exposed my backside to about 20 people who were in the waiting room. Hospital gowns suck! I only hope I didn't cause some of them to go blind. It was shortly after getting back to my room that the blood clot happened.

I gave a lot of seminars as a financial advisor and I always told my attendees to just say, 'No', if you don't feel well enough to get up and to not cave into the staff that operated under the policy, 'Treat 'em and street 'em'. The faster you're out, the more money they make. Just say, 'No'.

I love to cross-country ski. One of my favorite spots is Lolo Pass, which is 30 miles south of my home in Lolo. The pass is on the Montana/Idaho border. I left my house around 8:00 on March 4, 2006, to go skiing. The roads were really slick. I was driving a brand-new Subaru Outback. Halfway to the top of the pass, I saw a red Jeep lose control and slide across the road and come to a stop about six feet from going into Lolo Creek. I pulled over to help. There were three ladies in the car. The driver was spinning her tires trying to back up and away from the creek. The opposite was happening. She was getting closer and closer to getting in the stream. I got the driver's attention and told her what I wanted her to do. I asked the other two ladies to get out and help me push the Jeep away from the icy stream. I got the driver to ease off the gas and slowly back up. It worked, and in no time, they were out of danger. I asked them not to go anywhere for two hours, or until the road was sanded. They promised me they would not move, and as scared as they were, I believed them.

I have driven on that road well over 100 times, and I knew I could drive no more than 30 MPH and stay on the road.

I got to the pass and skied for about three hours. I loaded up to go home. On the way out, I stopped to help three little kids who were crying. 'Why are you crying?' 'We can't get our snowshoes on'. 'Where are your parents?' They pointed to the lodge. I started herding them to the lodge. Before we got there, out came the parents, bless their negligent little hearts. I told them I was happy to help their little ones get their snowshoes on. They didn't say thanks. Oh, well, I made the kids happy, and that's what counts. So, I did my second good deed for the day.

On the way home, I was following a ¾-ton pickup, driven by my friend who grooms the cross-country trails. He turned off the road about five miles down the pass. He liked to walk his dog on the way home. I drove on. I was past the bad turns and about 15 miles from home on a straight stretch when I looked ahead and saw a red car. I thought it was going way too fast. Concentrating on the road ahead, the next thing I saw was red coming at me, head-on! I remember yelling, 'Stop!', thinking how violent this crash is going to be. It happened in a split second. Two ladies were in the car that hit me head-on, going approximately 75 MPH. My airbag went off and it felt like someone punched me in the face. The collision knocked my new Outback about 40 yards. It took me several minutes to know if I could move. I thought I saw the driver's head move, so I knew I had to try to help her. I'm not sure how I got out of the car, but I did. I couldn't stand up, so I crawled on my hands and knees to their car. I grabbed onto the door handle and pulled myself far enough to look in the window. What I saw has given me nightmares to this day.

I was trying to crawl back to my car when a bunch of snowmobilers stopped to see if they could help. I asked them to go to the house across the road to call 9-1-1. Cell phones don't work in the canyon. One of them ran to the house. A few minutes later, another man stopped and helped me get back to my car, opened my back door, and managed to pull me into the back seat. Because I was shaking so badly, he put a coat over me. I wished I could thank these guys, but sadly, I didn't find out their names.

It was amazing how fast a Highway Patrolman arrived on the scene. There were eight other accidents on the highway that morning, but all were minor, so he came to my accident as fast as he could. I saw him go to the ladies' car to look in, and then he quickly came over to me. He asked me if I was OK, and wanted to know what happened. As soon as I told him, he said it was easy to see by the location of the car and the skid marks, that they lost control of their car and slid into my lane. Because I was shaking so badly, he said he wanted me to get into his car to warm up and wait for the ambulance and fire truck to arrive.

The fire truck arrived first, and they were worried that I was going into shock. They covered me in more blankets. The ambulance came soon after, and I asked them if the ladies were gone. I knew the answer. The ambulance person said they probably died on impact. I got into the ambulance, and they gave me some morphine. I've had it many times in the past. I'll be honest, I love the stuff! They took me to the ER at St. Patrick Hospital. They took a bunch of X-rays, to see if anything was seriously wrong with me, other than what is normally wrong with me. All I had was a small fracture in my back, and a lot of bruises on my upper body, especially where the seat belt was. My nose felt like it was broken, but it wasn't. I want to mention that the Highway Patrolman came to the hospital to see how I was doing. He knew that I was really upset. He told me that those two ladies were going to die that day, driving about 75 MPH and out of control. Maybe they would have hit a family and killed all of them. I have the highest degree of respect for Montana Highway patrolmen and women.

I didn't understand flashbacks until this accident. I saw that damn car coming at me at least 20 or 30 times a day, waking in a cold sweat for several nights. I can tell you that when someone dies in a car accident, it doesn't matter whose fault it is. Again, Jimmy Dixson haunts me and so does this accident. It took me two years before I could drive up the highway to Lolo Pass. Thank God they didn't put up two white crosses where the ladies died. People who put them up have good intentions, but for those who weren't at fault and lived, it's just a terrible reminder of what happened.

On Lolo Pass, four years before the car accident, I was snowshoeing up a mountain, south of the center. I started climbing in the dark, and it was about five below zero. As long as I was climbing, I was warm. I was packing my cross-country skis on my backpack. I planned on snowshoeing to the top, which was about a mile up, and then switching over to my skis, and ski down in my snowshoe tracks. I was about 200 yards from the top of the mountain when I heard a strange sound coming out of my body. There was a sharp pain in my hip. My left leg, where I had a hip replacement, was kind of flopping around. I knew the replacement ball had slipped out of its socket.

I figured my only chance to get off the mountain was to get my skis off, put them down on my snowshoe tracks, and try to slide on my stomach to the bottom. Getting my skis off was tough! It took a lot of time, and I was getting really cold, really fast. Stupidly, I didn't tell anyone where I was going, and to make matters worse, I picked a place where hardly anyone goes. I heard freezing to death wasn't such a bad way to die. I tried to slide down on my skis, and I went about 10 yards and rolled off them. It just wasn't going to work. I couldn't stand, so I figured, as a last resort, I would have to somehow have to crawl on my stomach all the way to the bottom. I knew my chances of getting to the bottom were slim to none.

I looked down and saw a snowmobiler coming up the road at the bottom of the mountain. He looked up and could tell I was in big trouble. He turned and came up the mountain as fast as he could. I told him about my flopping left leg. 'Can you get on a snowmobile'? 'No matter how much it hurts, I'm getting on it'!! Down we went and really, it didn't hurt as much as I thought it would. He gave me a ride to my pickup. I told my Good Samaritan that I thought I could drive myself into Missoula, to find my hip surgeon. I wrote down his name and wanted to pay him for saving me from freezing to death. He said, 'You're damned right! You owe me a fifth of Jack Daniels!'. I usually don't like most snowmobilers. I call them the 'Round people'. They create a lot of pollution, but this snowmobiler will always be one of my favorite guys. Actually, I have quite a few friends who snowmobile. I made it back to Missoula (my truck was an automatic!), then contacted my hip surgeon, and he asked me if I could wait until Monday to put my hip back where it should be? Then, I went home and said to my wife, "I'm going to walk by you, and you listen to this". She said, 'Oh, my God! I'll get your crutches', as walking was a bad idea.

Six years later, I felt a lot of pain in that hip. My original surgeon retired, so I called another surgeon who looked at the X-rays and said,

'You have completely demolished your hip! It looks like mush in there'. I said, 'Well, I had a really good time doing the demolishing'. The new surgery lasted almost seven hours, because they had to tie my joint together with eight cables. I sure didn't like the sound of that. This is the surgery that resulted in my getting a blood clot that just about got me.

I'm starting to get depressed, so I'm wrapping this chapter up. I've been hit in the head with a baseball bat, a hoe, a bowling pin, a lot of fists, several helmets, and a baseball. I'm pretty sure there are more missiles or implements that banged into my noggin, but hey! I'm lucky to be able to remember my name. My godmother, Montana Perriman, said, 'You Colbos are going to be really tough to kill!' I guess she was right!

Epilogue

Now, every day when I wake up, I think maybe I'm the luckiest man alive. I'm 81 years old. During my lifetime, I've had at least a dozen concussions where I have been completely knocked out.

I used to bench press over 400 pounds, but now, my shoulders prevent me from lifting very much. I'm in the twilight of a less-than-mediocre golf career. I still mountain bike pretty well, going downhill. I struggle going uphill. I solved that problem. I bought an e-bike. I cross-country ski as long as the snow isn't icy, and the temperature is between 35 and 38 degrees, with no wind and no possibility of being run over by a drunk snowmobiler. Oh, and no moose have been seen on the trail for at least five years. I play of lot of losing-chess. I have to find some new really dumb friends. I hike on easy, short trails, and even easier and shorter trails. Finally, I think I'll start writing another book on how to be happy doing 20% or less than what you used to be able to do.

Acknowledgements

First and foremost, I want to thank the best speller, the best grammar person and the best partner I could ever hope for, Judy (there were a couple of grammar things that she wanted to change, but I told her not to); Father Jack Murray, for his wisdom and guidance; My oldest daughter Kim, for countless hours of typing my scribbling; My daughter, Rachael, for being my hiking, biking and skiing buddy; Dan Gilman, for never forgetting any of our past adventures; J.D. Galiher, for letting me win one out of every ten chess matches, and putting up with my golf shenanigans; Dick Correll and Don Harbaugh, for being outstanding high school principals and human beings; Katy Huff, for always reminding me how special Butte people are; A special thanks to Mike and Penny Hegyi, for their outstanding computer knowledge, and for being the best neighbors anyone could hope for; John Waggonner, for being the glue that held all of us Sigma Chis together over the last six decades. Finally, my dog, Gracie, for not chewing up my notes!